Believe In Amazing

How Amazon is Changing the World
52 Emails to Jeff Bezos

Tom Matt

BOOMERS ROCK MEDIA, LLC
HOLT, MICHIGAN

Believe In Amazing

How Amazon is Changing the World
52 Emails to Jeff Bezos

BELIEVE IN AMAZING

HOW AMAZON IS CHANGING THE WORLD

by Tom Matt

ISBN-10:0-9855470-3-0

ISBN-13:978-0-9855470-3-5

First date of publication: March 2016

Cover graphics by Miranda Miller

Interior design by Mickey Hadick

Edited by Josh Raab

Published by Boomers Rock Media, LLC

www.BoomersRock.us

Believe In Amazing

Tom Matt

Table of Contents

PREFACE

In my soul I believe that at the foundation of greatness lies creativity. You may believe that creativity is some kind of inherent fixed trait, it is not. Think of a meandering stream that carries a leaf to the ocean, creativity is fluid, is dynamic and inspirational. You may think that some ideas are so outlandish that they are no more than fool's gold, that certain professions have more creative souls than others, they do not. Is a CEO, doctor or lawyer not as creative as an artist and architect or designer?

When you think of creative what do you think of?

In the 21st century we all, every generation, every race, every country, all people will need to harness the power of creativity, of ideas, of dreams to build a planet that endures, that inspires greatness, that unleashes unlimited potential. That was my intent with this book.

Creativity at its core is confidence, is a chance, is believing and conviction, and with it in our pocket we can change anything and everything.

Like a well-trained muscle our creativity and confidence to believe is up to us, each of us and all of us, because together we make a difference, together we have a shot.

Thank you for reading this book, and thank you Jeff Bezos for inspiring me to try. You inspired my creativity, now let's together make this happen!

Peace

1

LIVING WITH
"UNFUNDED LIABILITIES"

It is election season (or always seems to be), so I have been hearing this term Unfunded Liabilities, and as stated by Ben Carson May 4th, 2015 in the Washington Post, "It's not just the $18 trillion; it's the $211 trillion of unfunded mandates as well."

This is an issue worth sweating it out. Not to be a downer, but this black hole could swallow the world!

We always hear all kinds of new terms and issues being thrown around. This one, Unfunded-Liabilities, is one I want to talk about in depth, as it really gets my motor firing. And it should for you as well.

With two entitlement programs, Social Security and Medicare accounting for 47% of Federal spending today as reported by the Cato Institute, and the aging of America a fact, these programs alone are two of the biggest drivers of potential unfunded liabilities in the future.

I am convinced that the best way to deal with our nation's unfunded liabilities is for each and every one of us to deal with our own, personal, unfunded liabilities in health, fitness, happiness, and finances. I want us all to improve our quality of life.

If you borrow money from a bank, you are expected to pay it back. If you gamble at a casino on your credit card, you are expected to pay back your losses. The choices we all make in improving our quality of life, nutrition, active lifestyles, activities, connectedness and social engagements make borrowing or gambling less of a life altering black hole of debt. If you don't have the cash to pay back the loan, squander your credit on gambling, or have no intention of helping your friend, those are "Unfunded Liabilities" which will damage your relationship. A bank can harm your credit rating, and you might lose the friend; the gambler may bring some real hurt to collect the debt.

Ignoring debt can only make matters worse, head in the sand will not protect you when the tsunami hits the shore. Unfunded liabilities, entitlements, pensions and the like, started as great ideas. However moving forward into the future they have become the albatross around our country's neck.

We don't have to do it alone. We can help each other solve our own problems together. Friends help friends, neighbors help neighbors, and ultimately, citizens reach out to one another to improve our collective health, fitness, and finances. That will make a lot of us happy.

It is time to step up and fix things. Through adversity grows opportunity, I like to say.

I call this idea the Boomers Rock, (you may know, those 80 million or so souls born between 1946 and 1964), our 21st Century Deal.

We need to become engaged in the process of improving our QOL (quality of life), because our road trip is just beginning and we need all of the tools and supplies we can get to make this a memorable journey into the future.

What are these tools and supplies?

Here is the start of our list, and I would like everyone to contribute their own thoughts. No idea is a bad idea, (that's why it's called "Boomers Rock", not "Boomers Die"!).

I host a radio show and podcast called Boomers Rock. On the show, we have been building our collective mindset to think about our present and future finances with anticipation instead of dread. I do not like to talk negative on the radio show, so focusing our family of listeners and knowledgeable guests on the light of positivity improves our collective community. This is why I coined the concept of the "ReFirement Zone.". The "Igniting Your Life" and kicking "Retirement" to the curb is the mindset of all of us at the "Boomers Rock" nation. Now it's time to jump on the proverbial bus, make our voices strong, and find a seat, here we go!

Peace

Each chapter [of the ebook only] will include a link to a Best of 'Tom Matt's Boomers Rock Radio' talk show. For this opener I chose one of the best Psychologists I know, aging expert Dr Debra Heiser. This episode is titled "What's My Purpose", enjoy.

WEEK 1

Subject: Empowering others is cool

August 31st

From: Tom Matt

To: Jeff Bezos

Hey Jeff,

400 words or less, I promise!

In reading "The Everything Store" I felt compelled to share a quick glimpse of my plan to change the world. Why not, you did! As the youngest of the baby boomer generation you will like this, I am sure.

My name is Tom Matt; I work at Michigan State University by day, and as bootstrapped media entrepreneur, radio talk show host, author, and massive fan of Amazon by night.

From everything Prime to Kindle Fire, I believe that Amazon is amazing.

Please feel free to read my book and look at my account with Amazon.

Jeff, when I read you "attract people who pioneer and invent," I felt like David reaching out to Goliath for friendship. Your 'Amazon.love' memo convinced me that you will love my message, because 'thinking big is cool!'

I am all about relationships and quality of life.

Helping people will never go out of style. I would love to have the chance to interview you for my talk show "Boomers Rock.".

I call the show The Conduit of Good Information, and I am building a movement.

We launch our 4th season at the end of September on both internet syndication on 'VoiceAmerica' and in October on local AM radio 1370 WGHN, the talk show is the linchpin to the whole empire.

'Bootstrapped avocation', you gotta start somewhere!

I would be glad to send you my brain-map which illustrates the plan.

The tipping point of the generations is here, it is all about enlightenment and education. Tapping the $trillions of boomer accumulated wealth can improve society. With our experts we cover every discipline from science to art, business to politics, fitness to travel. If it has anything to do with living with maximized quality of life we talk about it.

Jeff my thought is this, if you keep customers alive, productive, and happy, isn't that a really good thing?

Let's talk about why 'YouTube' will never be a boomer thing, and why 'Amazon' will. Let's talk about how I believe the Kindle and reading is good for brain health and increase your odds of avoiding Alzheimer's. Let's talk about how customer convenience, service, and value fuel the boomer referral economy.

Let's talk, collaboration, Goliath helps David!

Peace

Tom

WEEK 2

Subject: Improve your Life Today!

September 7th

From: Tom Matt

To: Jeff Bezos

Hey Jeff,

Week 2 of the 400 words or less on topic of 'Quality of Life' as it relates to the 45 and older demographic, or as you said,

"How do you plan on handling the 'narrative fallacy'" of QOL and your customers, where do we go?

My answer, "many different ways," because of the 100 million or so people in the U.S. in this group, Goliath (Jeff) and Amazon, and the bootstrapped media mogul, David (Tom) and 'Boomers Rock

Today's conversation is one I discuss a lot: cognitive decline of a generation.

Heavy, yes, important, hell yes!

Jeff, I have had the pleasure of talking to some really knowledgeable doctors, specifically neuroscientists. The radio show gives me license to seek out experts and shoot the breeze. I like to refer to myself as a 'Cub- Scout' neuroscientist because talking about it and writing about it puts me in the unique space, therefore Cub-Scout Tom!

Specifically, doctors George Bartzokis and Gary Small of UCLA have been very kind to give me their time.

Generationally we have all have a BIG PROBLEM coming down the road, specifically dementia and Alzheimer's.

"At the current pace, Alzheimer's and other age-related dementias will strike more than 115 million people globally by 20501."

"Current research is largely aimed at slowing down the progression of the disease. Just postponing the onset of serious dementia by five years could reduce the number of patients by 43 percent and save more than $440 billion in caregiving costs, in the United States alone, according to estimates by the Rand Center for the Study of Aging2."

Put simply: "We've got to bring Alzheimer's to its knees, otherwise it will bring us to ours."

The biggest threat to our QOL comes in the form of disabling chronic diseases. Half of Americans over 50 now have a chronic disease that puts them at risk for disability, the U.S. Centers for Disease Control reports. Chronic disease is the precursor to cognitive failure.

We know the answer, and the answer to this is us!

As Doctor George Bartzokis told me, "Better odds Tom, we have to give ourselves better odds."

The Amazon one stop shopping 'value add' is to name just a few-

"Amazon's one stop shop is a perfect solution to our cognitive decline problem."

Balls of Steel!

Peace

Tom

WEEK 3

Subject: What's More Important to Baby Boomers Than Money

September 15th

From: Tom Matt

To: Jeff Bezos

Hey Jeff,

Writing this a day later than my self-imposed routine, (I could go into the psychology of chunking time here but I will save that for another well-deserved chapter), the weekend of the 'Invasion'.

Now I say this in a happy, although worn out fashion, the eldest daughter, son in law, and our first grand-baby daughter made their sojourn from Wisconsin this weekend.

Being semi-new to the grand parenting universe we take every moment with the little bundle of smilyness as a blessing, which it is.

Our daughter Ashley (we have two children, ten years apart, both girls and again more on that in anther note because the 'teenagerness', well it is enough to pull your hair out, again another time), after Ashley finished college relocated, in our neighboring Big Ten state of the land of cheese heads.

A wedding of one her friends gave us this weekend of togetherness.

My notes to you, Jeff, will always revolve around the added value to you and Amazon in my avocation of inside info on the boomer demographic.

Generational 'boomerness' is something that holds tremendous value for our society.

As you may now know, I share ideas with the sisters and brothers 45 years and older.

One thing I have learned as a grand-parent for the past 17 months or so, is that in our house you would do ANYTHING for the next generation, it really is the best.

We are not special, just 'averagely normal'.

A key term is 'Generativity.' I learned it from one of my best guests on the radio program, Psychologist Debbie Heiser.

To stay within my-self-imposed limit of 400 words here are some stats:

Grandparents

Jeff, providing a legacy for grandchildren is the next wave of investment and spending. College is one thing, but let me tell you day care adds up too!

Peace,

Tom

WEEK 4

Subject: Boomers and travel

September 21st

From: Tom Matt

To: Jeff Bezos

Hey Jeff,

In keeping with the theme of ideas that can change a generation, help Amazon and its market share, and rebuild the American dream, this week's 400 word subject is "Boomers and Travel."

It was interesting to read in Brad Stone's book, 'The Everything Store' the story of you and Amazon, that you had a scare in 2002 with that helicopter misadventure, sounded pretty hairy, funny how many parallels we boomers have with living life like a perpetual teenager and feeling indestructible.

Part of our problem, or it could be turned into a positive, is our free-wheeling mindset which sometimes leads to getting firmly planted on the couch injured, or in the ground, dead.

UGH!

From you, looking to build a launch pad for space exploration (go boomer go), to Richard Branson (another boomer) and Virgin Galactic, the level of interest in travel and adventureour generation has is massive.

Staying young at heart and in the brain is all about looking forward not back.

Planning a vacation, especially the multi-generational legacy type of sharing with family, is our generation's way of reliving our childhood.

Hell, we earned it, now let's share it!

From anniversaries, to birthdays, to destination weddings to entering the 'Refirement-Zone,' we boomers are never at a loss to have some fun.

According to my pal, travel expert Clark Norton , "travel, in general, does make us healthier and happier than those who don't travel, particularly as we age." Travelers, one study found, "report higher satisfaction with regard to their stress levels and their physical health and well-being."

He cited travelers' reports of beneficial effects on "mood and outlook" (86%); "stress level" (78%); "physical well-being" (77%); "mental stimulation" (75%); and "health" (70%) -- factors that should all lead to happiness. As Clark reported, these results from a study by the Global Coalition on Aging (GCOA) in conjunction with the nonprofit Transamerica Center for Retirement Research (TRCS) at the behest of the U.S. Travel Association.

It is a reality that Boomers are the most active, healthy, and wealthy generation of Americans in U.S. history. Our generation together controls more than half of all consumer spending and more than 80 percent of personal financial assets, according to some studies.

In terms of travel, boomers spend about 70 percent more on airfare than young travelers, twice as much on recreational activities while traveling, and about 2½ times as much on cruise ship fares and hotels, according to a recent Consumer Expenditures survey by the Bureau of Labor Statistics.3

Travel, it does a Boomer good!

Until next time, Bon Voyage my boomer brother!

Peace,

Tom

2

NURTURING THE NETWORK

Most parents reach a time in their lives when they no longer have to worry about raising their kids. The days of constant busyness, dealing with the active performer or athletic children/teens will eventually reach its conclusion; eventually we all will call our homes "empty nests".

This can be a very liberating or frightful period, it all depends on how we manage the time and our emotions, this gauntlet is called Empty Nest Syndrome.

As defined by Psychology Today the Empty Nest Syndrome "the feeling of depression, sadness, and/or grief experienced by parents and caregivers after children come of age and leaves their childhood homes. This may occur when children go to college or get married."

Personally, Sandy and I are living this right now. Our youngest is now off to college, and to be honest, it is an adjustment. Thank goodness we have been building the foundation and nurturing our network of activities, friends and projects. If you have not been building your foundation, fear not, here are some ideas that can enable your bridge to the next phase of life.

Your success is your job, be excited about the potential and LIVE! Peace

The featured radio best of this chapter is prolific women's health and fitness expert Joan Pagano. When Joan Pagano speaks, people should really listen. A wonderful lady, and long-term contributor to our radio program it endears me to talk fitness and women's weight training with the premier knowledge giver Joan Pagano. Enjoy this episode with Joan, she kills it!

WEEK 5

Subject: How can smartphones, portable devices change the practice of medicine?

September 28th

From: Tom Matt

To: Jeff Bezos

Hey Jeff,

Wearable tech, health, and the boomer: can smartphones, portable devices change the practice of medicine?

The changing outlook of the Baby Boomers as we reach what was traditionally viewed as 'retirement' is now defined by entering the 'Re-Firement Zone'.

Wearable tech is just another example of tools, for everything from fitness to blood pressure, from glucose levels to sleep, which can enhance our longevity.

Joseph Schumpeter stated that with creative destruction, "entrepreneurs will snatch markets from anachronistic precursors'." This was prescient, to say the least, as it applies to tech and modern QOL.

This year, the youngest Baby Boomers turn fifty years old. America is in the midst of a demographic upheaval, but this upheaval is about much more than longevity.

Our country is witnessing the emergence of a new stage of life between adult midlife – typically focused on career and child-rearing – and old age, customarily marked by increasing frailty and decline. This new stage of life spans several decades and is characterized by generally good health, relative financial stability, and an active, engaged lifestyle.

This is where through adversity grows opportunity, and 'ReFire-ies' live.

Dr. Eric Topol stated, "We'll soon use our smartphones to monitor our vital signs and chronic conditions."

Here are just a few items that will help keep more of us out of hospital beds.

And we haven't even talked about fitness devices, yet!. For example find these at Amazon:

Part of the problem is there is so much tech; I liken it to having 300 varieties of peanut butter, all good, but I am choosing Jif because I know and trust the brand.

Boomers are going to live a lot longer, the brand that I trust is, you guessed it, Amazon, and I look forward to telling my listeners to the radio program all about it.

Peace,

Tom

WEEK 6

Subject: The Boomers Rock Collective is coming

October 5

From: Tom Matt

To: Jeff Bezos

Hey Jeff,

As the boomers mature, several key factors will reshape America's marketplace for goods and services, because Boomers are going to live longer than any group ever has.

Centenarians will be the fastest growing demographic for the next 20-40 years, lifestyle choices, active living, with 78 million boomers, the youngest baby boomer is turning fifty this year, the age wave is just beginning. In 2000, approximately 605 million people were 60 years or older. By 2050, that number is expected to be close to 2 billion. At that time, seniors will outnumber children 14 and under for the first time in history. http://bit.ly/1KNp7LI

A 90 or 100 year lifespan will become commonplace. And as we search for the "fountain of health," boomers will try all sorts of things to stay healthy and young longer. Watch for growth in anything and everything that can forestall or minimize physical aging -- from joint replacement surgeries to vitamin supplements.

We changed majors in college and haven't stopped shape-shifting since.

Twenty percent have changed religions and 50% have changed spouses. Our appetite for trying new things and lifelong learning will not only propel the tech industry (for everything from mind-expansion software to smart homes), but will breathe new life into colleges and universities both as centers of adult learning as well as retirement housing meccas.

New adult life phases will require a wide range of products and services.

For example, the "empty nest" life stage will unleash an abundance of "discretionary time" – to be filled with everything from walking tours of Europe to cooking classes at the local Y. Experiences will be worth more than things

In an attempt to "live within our means" while trying to improve the quality of their lives, boomers will undergo a psychological shift from acquiring more material possessions toward a pursuit of enjoyable and satisfying experiences, fueling growth in the travel, leisure, entertainment and volunteerism sectors.

At the same time, the financial services industry will launch new products and services to help boomers "catch up" financially, manage more than $10 trillion of inheritances, extract liquidity from their homes, and mobilize practical saving and funding strategies to carry them through their long lives.

Years from now, historians will scratch their heads at an earlier American economy that focused for too long on the youth when the biggest untapped market -- men and women over 50 -- was hiding in plain sight.

400 or less, until next time.

Peace,

Tom

WEEK 7

Subject: A Bur Under the Cowboy's Saddle

October 12

From: Tom Matt

To: Jeff Bezos

Hey Jeff,

Would you consider yourself a 'senior citizen'?

Think about that for a moment, because it is the theme for this week's discussion.

As the boot-strapped radio talk show host we (my wife Sandy and I) take time from our careers (day jobs) to network with our new base of AM radio, Grand Haven, Michigan.

So, off we drive to meet the great souls who reside there. We had an opportunity this week to spend Wednesday spreading the news about season four of Boomers Rock. We spent time at our first sponsor's facility, 'Four Pointes', participated in Line Dancing, (never done before) and then meeting with 20 or so members of this facility.

Basically I would liken this place as a YMCA on steroids for people over 50.

Engaged and active people, by definition 'senior citizens,' but breaking that mold. Here is where we must define the antiquated term of 'senior citizen':

"People in the United States who are more than sixty years of age are commonly referred to as senior citizens or seniors".

Hmm, interesting, check this out, as the day progresses.

We move on our whirlwind meet and greet to the local Grand Haven Kiwanis luncheon, the speaker, a very active community member who heads the biggest event in the city in the summer, addresses the group with a story and refers to himself as a 'senior citizen', he can't be over 60.

Hmm, double interesting.

A magazine I now write a monthly column for decided to label my article in the category of 'senior'.

Ok that did it, time to step up and reconfigure the cognitive failure that has become our culture. I emailed the publisher and explained a couple of things to him.

In the 21st century people will decide how and what they are by doing what they do.

Make sense?

Redefining the old school mentality of aging is my game, but it is on you, the individual to be accountable. In our society today, people 45-75 are in midlife, which can lead to the ReFirement Zone occupied by 100 million or so people in the U.S.

You and I, Jeff, are 20 years or so away from 'Senior Status' (along with millions of others) and that is the point of my continued work.

Change the mindset, because life, it is all good.

My articles category in the magazine is now categorized as 'Boomer'.

That's better!

Peace

Tom

3

MAKING A RESOLUTION STICKY

"Lend yourself to others, but give yourself to yourself."
Michel de Montaigne

Did you set a New Year's Resolution last year? Did it stick?

It is that time again, the time when we are positive, resolute, and supposedly firm in our mission to set a life altering resolution.

Sound familiar?

Been here before? Are we going to do the same thing once again?

Resolutions are a fabulous, defined as, "a firm decision to do or not to do something" so why in a month do we fail?

We as Middle-Living baby boomers need a smaller goal, something more achievable. Use your brain to visualize your achievements, think yourself happier, and healthier. Setting realistic goals can be a starting point for a new habit, it will lead to your behavioral change 'sticking', and stickiness is directly proportional to small steps, it really is that simple.

Making your resolution too rigid, or too large will doom you to disappointment. We must rethink our plan.

Self-improvement is a perfectly doable goal. It is how we focus our energy that holds the key. Willpower is way overrated, and sets us up for failure.

Willpower cannot become sticky, behavior modification can. Believe in yourself, give yourself a chance!

Think sticky, think small change; think old cue, new behavior, new reward and new you!

Just because "I want to" does not mean "I have to," just because you are used to doing something does not make it permanent and just because it has always been that way does not mean squat.

Choose one of these:

Peace

This chapters best of features our financial fitness expert from Blue Mound Asset Management in Milwaukee, Wisconsin Kirk Spano. I titled this episode "The Optimistic Realist", because at times he can be!

WEEK 8

Subject: To Be or Not to Be, That is the Question

October 19

From: Tom Matt

To: Jeff Bezos

Hey Jeff,

"To be, or not to be..." is the opening phrase of a soliloquy in the "Nunnery Scene" of William Shakespeare's Hamlet.

The other day, on my daily commute to work, I heard a very compelling commercial delivered by Michigan's Governor Rick Snyder.

Compelling, that is, until the very end of the commercial, at which point I almost drove off the road and on to the sidewalk.

The commercial's message was one in support of "National Save for Retirement Week," a very commendable and laudable message to be sure, until our governor stated, (and I paraphrase), "retirement, the best vacation ever."

The perception and long held beliefs that 'retiring' is some kind of lifelong dream sequence of perpetual play or leisure is a marketing ploy devised in the 1950s to sell condos and encourage shuffleboard and golf. In 1999, AARP, the welcome wagon of retirement, dropped the word "retired" from its name. Ironically enough, many of its members are not 'Retired' but in fact working.

Recently, AARP created a new brand called 'LifeReimagined'.

Why is that?

The answer is that the attitude that perpetuates the thought process of 'retirement' only leads to an uglier monster, named "Ageism."

We have marginalized our older citizens, putting people into places of little or no value. Nowhere is that low value more clearly perpetuated than in the media. To portray older adults in mocking condescending humor clearly underestimates their wealth of talent and knowledge. This talent and knowledge is overlooked human capital!

Talent and knowledge is a value-add to our society!

The time has come to acknowledge the dignity of growing older in America. It is EMPOWERING, not weakening!

In other words "we are what we do, we are what we believe, and we are all full of potential greatness." This is walking into the ReFirement Zone

People between the ages of 45 and 75 exist as Middle Living adults, and people over the age of 75 continue to flourish in the well deserved senior citizen status.

The people who are in the Middle Living demographic are our country's economic engine in the 21st century. And our 'Seniors', they are in their own league, blazing trails, living!

Baby boomers alone hold the key to business growth and financial wherewithal. The Ewing Marion Kauffman Foundation found the share of new entrepreneurs ages 55 to 64 grew from 14.3% in 1996 to 23.4% last year.

The misperceptions that drive ageism is only enhanced by the Governor reading copy for a radio ad that is foolish.

What if the people of Michigan take the Governor's advice, save for 'ReFirement', and then take a lifelong vacation, out of Michigan.

That would be ironic and a waste of human capital, now wouldn't it?

To be or not, that is the answer!

Peace,

Tom

WEEK 9

Subject: The Circle of Life

October 26

From: Tom Matt

To: Jeff Bezos

Hey Jeff I hope all is well.

I still have the 'Senior Citizen' thing stuck in my mind as I drop you this note. I have many updates, everyday seems like a new adventure.

You may recall from last week's note that I dreamed up a new phrase that differentiates people not by the old school 'generational ' (Boomer, Gen-Y, Gen-X, Millennial) but into two categories for the demographics that I narrowcast the radio program toward

The 'Middle-Living' and the 'Senior'. Person's 45-75 are the Middle Living and those over 75 as the 'Senior'.

I was getting tired of the hard line between generations, when frankly the bottom line is this: If and when you reach 45, you better get your game face on, have a plan, start thinking about a plan, prepare for your plan, or don't whine about the issues that are stressing you out, because I guarantee you there WILL BE issues.

Step up, big boy/girl pants time!

The response I have had from some of my guests, colleagues, friends, pals is very positive, 'Middle -Living' is a winner!

So now that we have a better handle on all of this we need to continue and offer coaching, inspiration and give some thoughts and actions to keep people engaged, because it is the connectedness (can you feel the Amazon connection here) to people, life, jobs, and basically each other, that is going to make all of this work.

My next idea (again, imagine another creative lightning bolt) 'Boomers Rock U', where the 'U' stands for Unified. My friend David Hornak, principle at a local elementary school, and I are working on a pilot program now. We are going to use the radio program to promote awareness and interest in helping the school bring volunteers and even paid older adults, those in the Middle Living ReFirement Zone in and become part of a budgetary solution of extra bodies. They need the help and Middle Living adults need the engagement, win-win.

Build the model, polish the stone, and then roll it out.

The stabilizing effect of intergenerational relationships is a dynamic and needed societal paradigm. The disappearance of our 'village society', that is, the diminished feeling of responsibility for others' children, helicopter parents with fierce protectionism leads to less fluid encounters between generations perpetuating the ongoing angst of mine and yours.

Push the stone, polish the model, rebuild the village. You see the potential?

Change, collaboration, and community, it does the body, and does society good too!

The circle of life!

Peace,

Tom

WEEK 10

Subject: The 'Flywheel that is a Middle-Living Adult'

November 2

From: Tom Matt

To: Jeff Bezos

Hey Jeff,

This past week I was invited on a local radio program by a panel of local business experts here in mid-Michigan to discuss the 'Business of Boomers'. I was asked the 'what' question: What do Middle-Living Boomers want?

Wow, easy question!

Excellent health is number one, number two is acknowledgement and respect, which advertisers do not do. Middle-Living adults desire trust and love the soft sell.

Life is changing, it is more about the mindset of 'Generativity,' bling bling has become passé.

I read an article this week in The New York Times about your company, "Amazon's Grand Design For Devices" by Stuart Goldberg, and I found the dichotomy of Mr. Goldberg's opinion interesting. Flattering at some times, condescending at others. For example, "Amazon remains the best place online to buy books, movies, music and other media,", "Amazon's devices also highlight it's deep weaknesses." Critical of the Kindle Fire HDX he stated, "on paper, the HDX 8.9 sounds like a great deal, but using it is kind of 'meh'."

Wow! Who peed on his Wheaties?

Jeff your mantra of delighting users is spot on. Focusing on the invisible demographic that is the "Middle-Living" Boomers, cementing our reliance and brand loyalty to you is the way.

If Amazon is so 'focused on data' as Mr. Goldberg writes, why not focus on us?

Pitching to the Middle-Living Boomer demographic works like this: build trust and understand the customer's wants and needs. The spectrum of services and products is infinite. From home security, to the internet of things, retrofitting your house to age in place. Also delivery and transportation services are critical, the variety is endless.

For example, how many Middle Living adults in the U.S. have ever used 'Whispersync'? I have, love it, and show it off to people at my day job, gym, home and anywhere else. It is easy to use; love the compatibility, great for the brain.

An Amazon Home Run.

Everyone I show it to has never heard of it!

Middle-Living adults have parents, children, and grandchildren, the 'Heroes' of the sandwich generation, and the 'bling' has become so much 'meh'.

We will buy tablets because we want to show off pictures of our grandkids and read books, we want to Skype with them, we want to buy them Kindles and read to them, and maybe play their games.

Multigenerational relationships are the best!

We will buy a home security system, our groceries, a step through shower, and a smartphone but from whom?

Flywheel, culture shift and 'Generativity' data, Middle-Living data! Word limit, more later.

Peace

Tom

WEEK 11

Subject: If your life were perfect......

November 9

From: Tom Matt

To: Jeff Bezos

Hey Jeff,

If your life was completely perfect, what would it look like? Everyone is different; here is something to think about.

This week I had an opportunity to record a segment for the radio program with a woman named Anna Duggins, she is an attorney, Elder Law specialist and partner at a firm named 'Parmenter-O"Toole' located in Muskegon, Michigan. I had wanted to find an 'Elder-Law' expert for quite some time, and so Anna was a coup; we hit it off and the recording went fabulous.

If peeling back the onion of finding more components to the perfect life, 'Elder-Law' would be at the top of the peel.

To have the perfect life you need to have information, collaboration is the key. With the plethora of information that now saturates the world thanks to the Internet, everyone has a new, new thing.

The question is, can you have faith in that 'new, new' thing?

Remember from last week I shared thoughts on Amazon being the brand you can trust with 'big data'. The Middle Living adults are the invisible market and building trust is the key to capturing and owning our market. Appealing to the Middle Living demographic with a topic such as 'Elder-Law' is not only the right thing to do, it is a moral obligation. It is a trust builder.

Hello 'big data- trustworthy brand'!

As Anna and I talked after we concluded her interview, (this was just the high altitude view), all of the moving parts of Elder law clearly come into focus. It will be how we deal with the multitude of life's moving parts that will make the perfect life.

Data to the masses can be overwhelmingly boring to an end user, (sorry). Having your personal data protected, coordinated and organized in a fashion that benefits the next generation of heirs is dubious to say the least. However, everyone knows deep down we need to have a conversation about this.

For example what about end of life issues, what about probate, what about long term care, what about trusts and wills, Medicaid and Medicare, or placing your husband or wife of 40, 50, 60 years into a nursing home facility. Can you imagine the anguish?!

Emotionally draining and complex, the issues go on and on.

Remember the onion!

I hope you see the parallel to trust and big data. The century of the Internet will allow us to quantify every aspect of life; this is just one layer of our own onions quantification.

Helping others with these issues are bridge builders, they lead us into a place where we feel comfort, and in the end, it leads to the assisting of setting up the perfect life. The right data, the right way, will help people make the hard decisions and those decisions can help make the perfect life achievable.

QOL has many issues, finding coaches and building trust, long term and loyal is old school and it works!

You see my point?

Peace

Tom

CHAPTER 4

Be Super Successful, Think Transition!

"Success is liking yourself, liking what you do, and liking how you do it." --Maya Angelou

We Boomers have this dilemma, work hard your whole life and then...

Go relax is conditioning that was sold to our parents. For the Superior-Seniors, as I like to call them, this is not going to work for us Middle Living boomers.

Think about this, not giving up is a precursor to winning.

Looking into the next 30, 40, maybe even 50 years with renewed power and energy is the goal. Having a renewed sense of purpose, believing anything you ever thought possible is achievable.

Why then do we sometimes marginalize, disregard, and disrespect our own experiences? I believe it relates to experiences with past generations; the conditioning sold to mom and dad. Retirement was the golden ticket. Their belief was: "How could thirty years of experiences be of value to anyone, I'm old?" Today the statement is "how best to utilize your talents, and share them, because I add value!"

Cognitive dissonance is created by inconsistent thoughts, beliefs, or attitudes leading this harmful feedback loop I call the Negative Energy Tornado; it also fuels limiting beliefs.

Wasting valuable experiences and human capital is simply that, a waste!

I for one am done with that kind of thinking, it is positive transition into the ReFirement Zone. Let's develop a positive external image and attract new and exciting people into our lives!

Self-Improvement and positive expectations can begin at any time and any age.

Transition can be enhanced by accepting these beliefs:

Seek change as if you life depends on it, because it does!

I welcome your comments.

Peace

This chapters best of 'Tom Matt's Boomers Rock' radio shows is a perfect example of how we love to cover different categories in our outreach. Like many of the ideas in my emails to Jeff it takes a lot of creativity to live to 100, this show is on 'Dating After Fifty'- with expert author Lisa Copeland. Yes this episode is over the top, that's why we loved it so much, enjoy!

WEEK 12

Subject: Bigger Brother

November 16

From: Tom Matt

To: Jeff Bezos

Hey Jeff,

When over 91% of Americans are losing or have lost trust in the system of identity protection, 80% of Americans should be concerned about government's monitoring communications. Check out http://www.pewinternet.org/2014/11/12/public-privacy-perceptions.

Right to privacy is fading quickly and there is nothing we can do about it.

Who is going to step the frick up?

What if we had a omnipresent ubiquitous safety net, a filter, a bigger brother that was never going to let any bully kick our ass at school?

That or steal all of our shit, 'ReFirement' funds including, 401k, 403B, pensions, credit cards, bank accounts, life savings, house, girlfriend, wife, dog!

If you can create 'Echo,' I believe it is you!

Lack of control may destroy the trust in the Ecommerce world, that or the government getting involved in 'net-neutrality', whichever comes first, that great screeching sound is not the road Runner and Wile E Coyote falling off a cliff, it is potential of the 21st century flushing down the toilet.

Doomsday or Nostradamus, I think not, that is if 'Big-Brother' comes to the school yard to kick the crap out of the bully and scare away the boogeyman.

You gotta believe, and you gotta have trust.

We have had this 'trust' discussion before, it is big and it is real, but nobody is stepping up, why is that?

Last week it was examples of elder law,

The week before that it was Flywheel, culture shift and 'Generativity' data, Middle-Living data!

Four weeks ago it was wasting of human capital, and 'ageism'

And a while ago it was how in the 21st century people will decide they are defined.

Running from the bully does not solve diddly, you, my friend, have the potential to become the biggest of brothers in a completely cool and family sort of protection way.

Here is an excerpt from Jonathan (Jasper) Sherman-Presser and his blog about 'Echo':

"The dystopian world of the Echo advertisement is a near future (really, a present) in which no one knows anything, and everyone relies on a humanoid device to mediate their most intimate personal interactions--between parent and child, between husband and wife, between brother and sister.

Watching Amazon's Echo video this morning, I found myself wondering: what is Amazon's vision of the role that technology plays in society? And what is its view of the world we live in--and would want to live in?"

Hmmm,

I would love to have Amazon in our generations corner!

Peace,

Tom

WEEK 13

Subject: Connections

November 23

From: Tom Matt

To: Jeff Bezos

Hey Jeff,

This week I recorded an episode with Clive Thompson. You may have heard of Clive's work, he is a prolific tech expert and totally cool guy, been on the show numerous times.

It has always been part of the radio talk show game plan to include a tech category, being that with Middle Living adults and 'Superior-Seniors' thirst for QOL (quality of life), tech has a major impact.

One of the keys to living a prolific life is finding those sparks or catalysts, and the largest is connections.

Clive referred to "the phenomenon of multiples" where collaboratives embrace each other's work to come to that common solution.

Multiple sources have studied the effects of maintaining our connections and the inherent parallel to the QOL of older adults, (over 60). As people move forward in their lives they sometimes lose connections to friends, family, work, and social outlets.

Use it or lose it is a fitting way of thinking about this. 70% of how we age is dependent on choice, choosing to stay connected is incredibly important. The connectedness of the Internet offers massive potential.

Clive also talked about the "externalization of memory" and how we can enhance our QOL by tech helping us to remember. Clive was chatting up the prescription bottle tops 'glow caps' and the ability to allow tech to manage the complexities of prescription contraindication.

I have personally experienced this with my mother-in-law whose QOL has lowered by just such a situation. Multiple prescriptions for an elderly person, a 'Superior-Senior' (people 76 and older), and how the lack of monitoring of those drugs can destroy their life, as it did hers.

Drugs can take a 'Superior-Senior' and turn them into a 'dependent-despondent'; it is really sad and very common.

David Rose of 'Vitality' may have invented "Glow Caps", however there is always room for improvement with tech.

Older adults listen to talk radio, it is all about trust, and the conduit of good quality information.

We also chatted about wearables, and how estimates project that there will be some 80 million users of monitoring devices by 2016. I believe that number is woefully understated.

Clive referred to the Middle Living and 'Superior-Seniors' as having "crystallized intelligence." different than younger generations and their "fluid intelligence", being the savviest has its advantages, finding our 'big-brother' who will cut through the Internet's overwhelming abundance of information is all that is needed.

Remember what I said about "trust," younger entrepreneurs have not caught on, that is ok because we are going to make a difference, empowering our generation, and the rest is going to be history!

Peace,

Tom

WEEK 14

Subject: Why Do We Love?

November 30

From: Tom Matt

To: Jeff Bezos

Hey Jeff,

Time is the most precious of all resources, taken for granted until it is too late to change our future. Time is taken for granted in the busyness of our lives, it will be those who can shape time that can change the world.

Shaping time can be accomplished by love, loving more than yourself, giving to others, believing in the inherent good of the Earth, and all of the people who live here, in its beautiful natural evolution. By loving others you shape your time, you make your time infinite.

Only those who can see the sole purpose of life as an ongoing process, one of giving to others, requited love, special, will experience infinity, will experience magic.

Through the generations, through our giving the goodness of our souls, and sharing the mistakes that everyone is destined to make, can we teach our generations the way. The way that emboldens and extends and improves our quality of life, through that requited life of our relationships to others.

Many will search for years unable to fulfill the mission of love, unfortunate yet true. For some people the answer is always a riddle that cannot be answered, for some people it is unrequited love, other things become more important in their lives, for that I feel sorry for those poor souls.

However, the beauty of the world holds, the potential for anyone to see the light, and to find the love, that door is there for anyone and everyone to open. It is the storytellers and leaders who are unafraid to share their personal trials and tribulations that can enlighten the path.

Stories can inspire, actions can change, and shape destinies, giving to others is of paramount importance because the world is thirsty for examples and enlightenment, empowerment can begin at any time.

Having just spent a couple of days with my eldest daughter, and her first daughter, my first granddaughter has empowered me to write this short passage. It is through the simple fun times of living and growing, giving part of your soul to the next generations.

It is an investment of your time, that finite resource that can live forever if you share it in the right way.

Time may be finite, but love can convert time into a limitless resource, magical.

It really is about inspiring people to never give up, ever!

I hope you and your family had a great Thanksgiving holiday, looking forward to talking to you.

Peace,

Torm

WEEK 15

Subject: The 'Linus Project'

December 7

From: Tom Matt

To: Jeff Bezos

Hey Jeff,

Virtually every email I have sent to you has included the concept of 'trust', today we bring 'Linus Van Pelt' of the comic strip 'Peanuts' into our conversation. More importantly and to my theme it is 'Linus' and his famous 'Blanket, and how I see a perfect match in helping the world become a safer, better place.

Think of it as Amazon's new service called Linus.

Jeff I am sure you remember that Linus used his blanket in many ways, first introduced June 1st, 1954, as primarily his 'security' blanket it had many uses over the years-

Linus' blanket in Peanuts has the ability to be reshaped into nearly any form and be put to many different uses. These are:

The Internet and all of its magic carries with it a dark side, the lack of security. We Americans are constantly reminded of theft of personal information, intrusion, and lack of trust.

Nothing will usurp the effectiveness of e-commerce more than losing trust in the system. Protecting our heirs and their legacy is critical to the Middle Living and Superior-Senior populations. Baby Boomers in the United States biggest retirement-related fears are a combination of health and financial concerns, including personal security.

Bank of America's Sarbjit Nahal and Beijia Ma write that boomers are expected to transfer some $30 trillion in assets to their heirs over the next 30-40 years in just the U.S. There are a lot of unscrupulous people who would love to take advantage of older adults and their legacies.

Amazon already has my business as a 'Prime' customer, why not become the '21st Century security blanket', just like Linus, he showed us had many unique potentials and uses.

For example 'Linus' could monitor any and all of our routine daily practices, the moving parts of life providing unparalleled protection and coordination.

Blanket coverage through the 'Linus Life Line from Amazon'. Remove the fear, inspire trust.

Please listen to a podcast of the show sometime, trust starts at many levels, especially grassroots.

Peace,

Tom

5

THE LATE BLOOMER-BOOMER

"I am the master of my fate, I am the captain of my soul"
Invictus-
William Ernest Henley
When Diana Nyad swam from Cuba to the U.S. on September 2nd 2013, a distance of a 110 miles, in 52 hours and 51 minutes at the age of 64, she proved to the world that dreams, however impossible they seem, can come true.

Colonel Harland Sanders started the Kentucky Fried Chicken franchise in 1952 at the age of 65, driving across the country cooking and selling his famous chicken. If the restaurant liked his fried chicken, he entered into a handshake agreement that stipulated a nickel for each chicken sold. By 1964, he had franchised more than 600 outlets. That year he sold his company for $2 million.

Finishing my college education later in life, 46 for the undergraduate degree and 49 for my Master's degree was not closure of a chapter in my life. It became the catalyst to the next phase; my personal 'Late Bloomer-Boomerness'.

You too can become a successful Late Bloomer-Boomer. It will not be magic, it will be an adventure. It will involve taking incremental steps and risks. Maturing is a process that enables us to become emotionally and mentally stronger. Having endured life's trials and tribulations our journey to self actualization involves an enhanced sense of pride. It is not so much ego driven as our ego being involved.

It is our time to relinquish our comfort zone and grow. My friend, author, and jobs expert Kerry Hannon calls it her "Hover Approach". It has five basic elements which are: Hope, Optimism, Value, Enthusiasm, and Resilience.

Being a Late Bloomer-Boomer is an opportunity to grow, use these tips to be successful-

Peace,

This chapters best of 'Tom Matt's Boomers Rock' radio shows is a another sample of how we love to cover different categories in our outreach. Derek Sivers, one of the most prolific entrepreneurs, pro-grammer, writer, entrepreneur, avid student of life joins the show and what an episode it is! The big take away here, like much of the book material is never giving up, enjoy!

WEEK 16

Subject: Fighting for your Life

December 15

From: Tom Matt

To: Jeff Bezos

Hey Jeff,

One curious observation I have is that certain people are not willing to stand up for themselves and do what they must to live the life that they deserve, they just settle.

Why is that?

Becoming aggressive is not in some people's nature, I get that, however, when it comes to your life, what else is there? Don't be accepting or passive, get motivated, become inspired.

I searched for a very long time to try to find the silver bullet of motivation, that trigger, the external or internal catalyst that I could coerce. Read all of the books, talked and interviewed psychologists, and still I was frustrated by the lack of ability to be that coach or trainer who could will someone to want to change.

It does not work that way.

I interviewed a very educated leadership expert a couple of years ago and asked her the question, "how do you motivate someone to change?"

Almost like a lightning bolt she answered with such energy and clarity, "Tom, you cannot motivate a person to change, motivation is intrinsic, what you do is you inspire a person to become motivated, you are a very inspirational person."

Wow, sometimes when the answer becomes clear it becomes so simple that you laugh at the thought that it was so complex, when really it was so simple. Like a hard geometry problem in high school, magic.

I feel we have an obligation to try and inspire others to engage every fiber of their being to live. You must fight for your life, you must appreciate the gift that you own. Some may see the world in a spiritual vein, or religious dogma or the science of quantum physics, whatever you please, the bottom line is your responsibility to give it your damn best effort and not whine, bitch or moan.

Do the best, help others, be kind, be loving, don't screw people over, and karma will smile upon you.

Everyone has an obligation to not wait for some big brother or government handout, not to bemoan the woe is me mindset.

Fighting for what is right, fighting for your life, fighting to improve the process, fighting to fulfill the dream is noble.

I have heard that after three years, if a business has not made any money than it is not a business it is a hobby. Being a fan of Malcolm Gladwell I believe in outliers and that it takes ten years to become an expert.

You gotta do what's right and fight for what is right.

Peace

Tom

WEEK 17

Subject: The 'Nest' Egg

December 22

From: Tom Matt

To: Jeff Bezos

Hey Jeff,

October 2014,The Fast Company Magazine cover pictured Tony Fadell with the words "The 3.2 Billion Dollar Man"

Quote from article from Tony Fadell:

"In this connected age, no company can stay bound to 'I'm just going to make this piece of the puzzle.' You're seeing Samsung, Google, Apple, Amazon, and Microsoft all trying to do it. If you're just trying to package Android in a better way, you're not thinking about the entire experience. That's where the reinvention happens."

Hmmmm

I like the word reinvention, but I love the word relationship so much more.

It is the trust (one of my favorite terms in my notes to you, Jeff) that builds the relationship.

Quick story:

From 2006-2009 I was enrolled in a graduate program at Michigan State University, not a big deal except that I was 46 years old when I started and I had just finished six years of undergrad work. Ok, so I took a little sabbatical on my way to academic excellence, like 20 years, better late than never. The biggest thing I noticed being the father figure in my program and just a couple years younger than my adviser was: Traditional students, all very bright, super smart and downright intimidating, had this one major weakness, interpersonal skills.

Being the dad in my classes helped me to overcome my anxiety, and it helped propel me through my program. As soon as I figured out that you are worthy, and even the brightest of light bulbs can use a little help in the world of illumination, relationships build trust, and trust builds empires!

And older students overuse metaphors!

Now in the connected world, and dealing with our demographic of Middle Living adults I have another story.

Recently when I met a group of people at Four Pointes, one of my sponsors for the radio program, I asked a small group what they would like to hear on the radio program, what categories? Several people offered suggestions, for example 'aging in place', 'financial issues', 'exercise tips', I told the group no problem, we have all of that and more. Then a person stated "well what if I am busy on Saturday morning at 9:00am when the show airs, how can I hear it?"

"No problem, we always have the podcast, you can listen whenever you would like," I triumphantly replied.

Jeff, the glazed over look was kind of startling until one member asked "how do you spell Podcast"?

It is not the device or the service Jeff, it is understanding where we can help and build trust. No different than understanding the issues with the traditional student or the issues with a Middle Living adult. It comes down to where can we educate and help people see the value. It all starts with trust and relationships every time!

If you cannot empathizes with a person's lack of knowledge, their insecurities, their feelings of inadequacy, then you miss the market.

However, if you do, you will own it!

Fadell's 'Nest' might be good, Amazon on the other hand is already great, see my point.

Peace be with you and happy holidays. Thank you for what you do to make my life better.

Tom

WEEK 18

Subject: The Inner Voice

January 4

From: Tom Matt

To: Jeff Bezos

Hey Jeff,

William James defined religion in his The Varieties of Religious Experience as not a particular theological doctrines, but rather as "the feelings, acts, or experiences that help one understand whatever one considers divine."

To me that kind of says it all, I have always liked Einstein's "Spooky action at a distance" quantum physics entanglement theory. Malcolm Gladwell refers to it as 'Thin Slicing'.

The world is filled with examples of miracles and craziness, I love it!

On January 10th, 2014 on a radio episode I conducted with my financial fitness guru Kirk Spano I predicted the stock market would hit 18,000 in 2014 (link here) it is only a little more than 2 minutes into the episode if you care to listen.

Was it spooky science, religious fortitude, great guess? No it was faith. Faith that everything in our world is going to improve, that people will improve, economies will improve, everyone will benefit.

Is it going to be magic or thin slices? Hardly!

Never one to dismiss positive attributes, I have been told I possess a very high level of what my pal and highly successful motivational speaker Chris Johnson call 'juice'. For the longest of times I never really understood this thing called 'juice', but the more I do what I do it has become clear.

Juice is the best, and we all need more people to drink it.

This is where being a spooky science fan comes into play, quantum physics, divine intervention, whatever floats your boat, you gotta drink the 'juice'. You must believe in something and have faith that with the right mindset, the right confidence, the right examples, you too can become great.

Yesterday my microphone decided to die, last night I had a dream I was unemployed and doing talk radio no one listened to, writing books no one would read, sharing ideas of greatness and self improvement, and everyone thought what a fool that guy is.

You know what I did when I woke up? Thought about the dream, remembered about my microphone, got on my computer and ordered a new mic (from Amazon) and proceeded to my basement gym to get the work out in. Shaking off the negativity of dreams, broken microphones and having confidence in my pals at Amazon puts everything in perspective, that and giving time to yourself in positive actions.

Rabbi Harold Kushner wrote, "Suffering in and of itself is meaningless; we give our suffering meaning by the way we respond to it."

That is a recipe for divine intervention, s*i* happens. Self improvement is personal, as is faith.

You gotta be ready for the juice.

Keep the faith, I read that Amazon has had some quarterly difficulties, fear not because karma is coming your way.

You gotta believe, I do!

Peace

Tom

WEEK 19

Subject: How Do You Measure Your Life

January 11

From: Tom Matt

To: Jeff Bezos

Hey Jeff,

Well, as usual on my way to reading several books at once, I became enthralled with an author, go to Amazon and buy another book. This time, again, with Whispersync. The funniest thing though is that as I get ready to write this note I decided to look through your book again, 'The Everything Store', find a couple of lines I had highlighted and move on to my writing desk to write my letter.

I found a couple of passages, and then I came across another on page 234. All I had underlined was 'The Innovators Dilemma'; I read how you and your team had devoured this book. The two books I am now reading, Dr. Clayton Christenson's 'The Innovators Dilemma' and the book I referenced earlier, 'How Will You Measure Your Life'.

Bizarre, string theory, spooky science, or just kinda cool, but to buy that book yesterday leads me to the writing of this week's letter. Look it up, I bought both from you.

Now you wrote your 'Amazon.love' note (pg. 317) and you reminded everyone how you wanted your company to conduct itself and be perceived by the world.

Value and determination, great stuff, how is that working out? The reason I ask is that many successful companies could care less about something like that, why you? Is it the lesson learned in Dr. Christenson's book? Disrupters always comes in from nowhere to rock the world?

I believe that over complicating things is a Middle Living person's one-one thing. It is our next move unfortunately. Those that can see forward far enough to understand that 'How You Measure Your Life' is all about learning and giving back, will prosper. Those people that cannot see forward simply retire, sit on the porch, and succumb to an outdated, and habitual ritual of dying alone and unhappy.

Sad but true.

Dr. Christenson has his paradigm, "that disruption happens when a competitor enters a market with a low-priced product or service that most established industry player's view as inferior. But the new competitor uses technology and its business model to continually improve its offering until it is good enough to satisfy what customers need."

You see without you building Amazon and then the Kindle I would never have started reading 'How Will You Measure Your Life?' by Dr. Clayton Christenson yesterday.

Changing the world is doable, if you think like a disrupter, do great work and have passion.

Someday we will chat, that I am sure of.

Peace,

Tom

6

BE STRONG!

Whom-ever said, "No Pain, No Gain" never had chronic pain!
- Amanda Lakso

For two years I had been dealing with a nagging knee injury, not enough to keep me down, but enough to remind me that something was not right.

My quality of life suffered.

Chronic pain doesn't just hurt your body, it hurts your emotions. If you let it, it can impact your mood, your memory, your relationships, Don't let it.

Chronic pain can diminish concentration, memory, critical thinking abilities, and productivity. It's hard to stay on your game at work when you're in constant pain. Don't give into it.

It was up to me to have my game face ready. Getting a second opinion only confirmed what my initial doctor had said, but getting the second opinion was critical to my decision to be strong and get it fixed. Get a second opinion!

I am here to say that I was afraid of being laid up, and that was foolish. When you have an injury, or suffer from chronic pain, do not give into the mindset that as we grow older chronic pain is part of life. It is not, and it is up to you to make the decision to man or woman up. If you hurt, do everything you can to fix it.

Peace

This chapter of the irreverent radio talk show best of is the topic of 'Elder Law'.

Complex, deep and very important I found that having attorney Katie Lynwood as our guest not only answers questions, but also fills in the blanks. Please listen to this episode if you have any questions regarding the topic of Elder Law.

WEEK 20

Subject: The Leadership and the Wellness Paradigm

January 19

From: Tom Matt

To: Jeff Bezos

Hey Jeff,

I am working on a presentation for a group that meets monthly at the University where I work. They discuss many different topics, mostly management oriented. I threw my hat in the ring to volunteer for this, not only to work on my public speaking skills, practice always makes perfect, but to share my views on a topic which is important in all organizations: employee wellness.

How can we improve the organization as a whole through individual wellness?

Like a family, sometimes we have this idyllic image of what we would like our organizations to be.

Happy employees show up for work eager to perform their jobs and give 110%, cruise through a very productive day, return home, and rinse repeat daily. We wish this was the case every day.

Our business practices are perfect, right?

And yet we struggle, and wish for this lofty goal. How to achieve this heavenly dream?

It is the culture shift of leadership through the wellness paradigm.

Like a poorly designed New Year's resolution, changing behavior on a large scale is a plan destined to fail. Breaking down the problem into manageable steps can be done, but it starts first at the top and trickles down to the bottom.

Gravity has a natural way of shaping everything, look at the Grand Canyon for example.

I love the definition of culture by MIT's Professor Edgar Schein:
"Culture is a way of working together toward common goals that have been followed so frequently and so successfully that people don't even think about trying to do things another way. If a culture has formed, people will autonomously do what they need to do to be successful."

Leaders begin the process by walking the walk and inspiring the talk, this is group learning and the beginning of the culture shift. If the wellness paradigm is to be successful, it has to be empowering.

Loving your work starts with inspiration and attitude. Are you buying in or not? Do the leaders lead by example and let the actions and behaviors do the talking? Are we encouraging the wellness paradigm through a culture of positive behaviors?

Doing the little things can add up to a large improvement, it is no different than your personal goal of losing twenty pounds or putting in more time at the gym. Build awareness and shift the culture, do the little things a tad bit better. Challenge leaders to own their personal wellness and watch them feel better, react better, lead better.

Trickle down starts with a raindrop from the clouds. Donuts in the break room make fat sluggish people.

A culture of excellence begins by taking accountability for yourself, there is no other way.

Empowering, yes, fun, for sure; when you believe in your own greatness, magic can occur.

Oh, and speaking of the organization, the family, our success is maximized amplified and profitable.

Happier, healthier leadership is the foundation of success, I guarantee it.

Peace,

Tom

WEEK 21

Subject: The Mentor

January 25

From: Tom Matt

To: Jeff Bezos

Hey Jeff,

One of the advantages of hosting a radio talk show is learning about quality of life issues and creating a network of influence. Having license to reach out to people like you, for example, is fun and many times, if the guest wants to come on the show we, become pretty close.

This is how I learned intensive details regarding Alzheimer's I found a mentor who is the coolest of the cool. I've already brought him up in these letters, Dr. George Bartzokis of UCLA.

Alzheimer's is the defining condition for our generation and it is a plague. It can ruin families and completely obliterate a whole family's quality of life. In the very first phone call I ever had with Dr. George four or five years ago he asked me in his pan-European accent:

"Tom, how old are you going to be"?

Sensing the trap door of the question, I responded kind of nervously,

"Well Dr. George, if you are asking me that question it cannot be good, but my answer is 100".

His reply was another question, "Ok, then what do you think your odds of developing Alzheimer's"?

Another nervous response, "50 percent"

His response, "try 80,"

Ugh, that sinking feeling of learning something that maybe you did not want to learn.

This whole conversation led to the beginning of our relationship and made me become an advocate of his work, sharing the passion for giving yourself better odds of not being in the eightieth percentile!

Understanding the proverbial what and why of Myelin, Dr. George's work is simply electrifying. We developed a strong relationship and I asked him if he would be so kind as to mentor me in sharing the Alzheimer's condition on the radio show, he agreed.

See this link- http://www.sciencedirect.com/science/article/pii/S155252600700026X for details about his pioneering research.

One of the greatest fears of Middle Living adults and the Superior Seniors, those who are our parents, is losing their sense of self, becoming lost , is how other experts have described the condition to me.

There are ways to help ourselves to gain some ground on this, better odds as my mentor said, outreach and education is the key.

I reached out to Dr. George in December to come back and record another segment, and had not heard back. Since he travels so much I knew I would eventually because I always had before. While doing some work on our archived shows on the website I came across one of Dr. George's recordings, and wanted some new bio material, so I Googled his name for some new information.

Dr. George Bartzokis my mentor and visionary researcher died of Pancreatic Cancer on August 22nd, 2014 after a short illness, he was 58 years young.

I was shocked to say the least.

Jeff we have to encourage everyone to believe in the greatness of life, that stories like this happen all the time. I feel blessed to have had the privilege to learn and discuss life with this great man.

Becoming part of the solution, helping share the word, inspiring is the way.

Changing the world is possible, I know it, you just gotta give yourself the best odds!

Peace

Tom

WEEK 22

Subject: The Primest and the Bestest

February 1

From: Tom Matt

To: Jeff Bezos

Hey Jeff,

Congratulations!

According to the Friday edition, January 30,2015 of USA Today Money section Amazon had a 'modest profit' in the fourth quarter. Their statement, first paragraph, "but it left open the possibility more losses will follow," is backhanded slap!

Do these articles just bug the shit out of you? Because they do me, and I am just a loyal customer who frankly loves Amazon, (read 21 previous emails, with 30 more to finish my quest, digress, so sorry).

Basically what do you have to do to please these knuckleheads, skydive out of a jet without a parachute like Captain America? I mean, really, do they search for the slimmest of ephemeral news to pounce and dig, stab and throw under buses?

Back to positivity, and my weekly message from the land of Middle Living/Superior Senior avocationist talk show host. (Yes, avocationist is not a real word, but when you compare to 'possiblity of more losses,' I think you see the point).

I find it interesting that your Prime customers, all 40 million (me included) helped drive your profits according to the article.

We all thank you for the services rendered and do appreciate it. Why would we not pay for our yearly membership with all of the benefits?

My question to you is this: if you have 40 million members, which obviously we are happy with forking over a $100 a year, and those members spend an average of $1500 and non-members spend on average $625, then sharing the multitude of bennies would behoove you guys, right!

So here is this week's idea, and of course it relates to my talk show demographic and your 'Amazon Prime Pantry'.

First I applaud you for having this service, and forgive me for being a no-nothing about it. That in essence is the point.

If I, lover of Amazon and long term Prime member, had no clue about 'Amazon Prime Pantry,' how many others like me are there in 'Prime' land?

Sandy, the earlier mentioned consternated wife, is a coupon saving machine, I love her dearly, so I have her evaluating your 'Pantry' and her opinion will grace another of my 30 future letters.

Anyway- 'Amazon Prime Pantry' meet 'Meals on Wheels' you two need to become acquainted.

When Meals started in England during World War II, it was there to assist mostly housebound elderly, and to this day continues to be a vital service in our country for those unable to cook or shop for themselves. Eight million meals served since 1974, over 323,000 meals since 2013/14, superb would be an adjective that is insufficient.

The global aging phenomenon:

By 2040, the proportion of people over the age of 65 will top 20 percent, and people under the age of 18 will make up almost 23 percent of the population. As a result, the oldest and the youngest populations combined will make up almost half of all U.S. residents.

https://www.planning.org/research/family/briefingpapers/multigenerational.htm

Aging in place, in your home, is what reportedly 90% of people want to do. It is enhanced by having a sustainable source of food and healthcare products. Aging in Place meet 'Amazon Prime Pantry,' nice to make your sustainable acquaintance.

Discounted Prime membership for Superior Seniors, networking with a small town middle America, avocation driven talk show host, $1,500 compared to $625 and a population of Middle Living-Superior Seniors reaching close to 175 million, hmm, just thinking!

The 21st century is not the 1950s!

For more info on 'Aging in Place' click on the link.

Through adversity grows opportunity, Jeff, my man, and the thought of 'more losses' can evaporate forever.

We booming Middle Living adults, you and I and 100 million others, yep we gotta blaze trails, and keep those revenues up and we gotta think big, Amazon and the world big.

The job of a leader is to rally people toward a better future! Welcome to a better future, led by Amazon Prime Pantry!

Peace,

Tom

THE FIRST REPLY!

Amazon.com Executive Customer Relations <orders4@amazon.-com>

2/2/2015

Dear Tom ,

Thanks for taking the time to write to us with your feedback.

We want to provide service on a level customers will remember, and it's great to know we've succeeded. I'm sure to forward your feedback to the appropriate team. Please know we love to hear our customers feedback and thoughts on how we are performing.

We really value your inputs and are always happy to hear our customers' thoughts on how we can improve the services we offer. We're constantly fine-tuning our presentation to provide our customers with the greatest value, selection, and information for their online purchasing decisions.

Tom, thanks again for taking the time to provide this feedback to us.

Regards,

Madhu P.
Executive Customer Relations
Amazon.com http://www.amazon.com
=

WEEK 23

Subject: Amazon Prime-Example

February 8

From: Tom Matt

To: Jeff Bezos

Hey Jeff,

So I heard from someone at Amazon on my last letter, that was encouraging and exciting. I thank the staff who probably gets hammered with email, I had faith, believe in you and your team.

Idea number 21!

This week we steer in a different direction slightly, another thought and idea and another way to maximize helping the world and Amazon at the same time. I call this one 'Point Guard'.

According to Wikipedia: "A point guard has perhaps the most specialized role of any position. They are expected to run the team's offense by controlling the ball and making sure that it gets to the right players at the right time. Above all, the point guard must totally understand and accept his coach's game plan; in this way, the position can be compared to a quarterback in American football."

In our society, the U.S. and the world at large, we are reaching the tipping point of an aging society. The numbers of Americans ages 65 and older will more than double over the next 25 years, reaching 80 million in 2040. The number of adults ages 85 and older, the group most often needing help with basic personal care, will nearly quadruple between 2000 and 2040.

With 14% of people 65 and older with no savings whatsoever, and with the largest transfer of wealth ever occurring in the next 25 years, estimated at $12 trillion there is going to be a lot of shaking going on as the song says.

Positioning is everything.

Time for a new point ally to emerge, it is called Amazon's 'Prime-Example'.

In last week's letter I talked about how I love being a 'Prime' customer and how your 40 million of us not only spend more money at Amazon, almost 2-1, but how a sustainable model could be created with your 'Prime Pantry'. This next step is the logical evolution into the 'Prime' club.

'Prime-Example' is a hybrid model of the sharing economy that is now all of the rage; with the younger demographics that is. The above mentioned non-savers in the older generations may not have saved a lot of money, but what they have done is acquire a lot of experiences, stories, and stuff.

Together we maximize a take-off on the 'sharing economy' for older Americans, we enable-

A new idea, a pipeline that brings great PR to Amazon for being at the forefront of assisting the millions who think they have not saved when in fact they have a gold mine of experiences, assets and abilities.

Amazon 'Prime-Example' enhances membership, and gives hope to millions!

With the new 'Point-Guard' directing traffic, advising, facilitating, older adults who don't have a clue about the 'sharing economy' soon will because they have more than anyone to share. But you have to be a member, you follow the lead of the point.

So much more than eBay, Amazon 'Prime-Example' is a game changer.

Not having savings is a bad thing obviously. However, programs that can put money in people's pockets by joining an exclusive club, and get rid of 'things', sharing experiences, memories, writing books can be done. You just need a point-guard to drive the team bus.

"In a dark place we find ourselves, and a little more knowledge lights our way"

Yoda

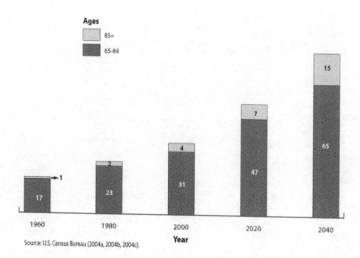

Number of Older Americans, 1960-2040 (in millions)

Source: U.S. Census Bureau (2004a, 2004b, 2004c).

"Refuse to express a passion and it dies," wrote eminent Psychologist William James. I write to you because I have ideas, thoughts, and a passion to make a difference. You must build alliances, friendships and loyalty.

Show people you care, be creative, outrageous and never quit, that is how I roll.

Peace,

Tom

THE SECOND REPLY!

Amazon.com Executive Customer Relations <orders4@amazon.-
com>
2/10/2015
Dear Tom,

Thanks for taking the time to write to us with your suggestions.

I appreciate sharing your thoughts about 'Prime-Example'. I can tell
you've given this a lot of thought, and we're grateful you took the time
and opportunity to send us your ideas.

We are always happy to hear our customer's feedback on how we can
improve the services we offer. To ensure your idea is reviewed, I've
shared your comments with development team for their consideration
when planning future improvements.

Please feel free to continue to send us any suggestions for improvement as your opinion and participation is valuable to us.

We look forward to serving you again soon. Best wishes and thanks
for choosing Amazon!

Regards,

Madhu P.
Executive Customer Relations
Amazon.com http://www.amazon.com

7

LEADING THE WAY

"Some people want it to happen, some wish it would happen, others make it happen".
Michael Jordan

In a recent article in the Wall Street Journal, Sara Germano wrote that, in a survey from the Physical Activity Council 1 in 4 Americans did not exercise at all in the past year.

Yes, according to the article 25% had not done any type of exercise, AT ALL!

As I like to say on the radio program, "through adversity grows opportunity." It sounds like it is time for the Middle Living/Superior Senior demographics to lead a new mindset. We need to teach, instruct, and lead by example in the area of fun, and activities that promote movement.

How will we do this?

By leading by example and walking through the front door of the "ReFirement Zone"!

The number of completely sedentary Americans has risen 18% since 2007. Experts are concerned that decreasing minutes for gym class in schools is a chief contributor to rising levels of inactivity among those children as adults.

Ever heard of 'Tag' or 'Red-Rover'!

'Athleisure,' really is a word, I looked it up and received 203,000 responses in .37 seconds. It is the hottest trend in Los Angeles where a pair of $600 'track-pants' (I think we used to call them sweats), is normal and pretending and looking like you're active is now the cool, trendy thing.

When the 'athleisure' clothing market has become synonymous with looking sporty, while not actually doing anything, it is time for all of our tribe to actually sweat in our new warm-ups and cool looking sneakers, (which speaking of expensive sneakers the Air Jordan 11-Blackout are a bargain at just over $11,000!)

Time to lead; how many of us remember playing touch football in the street, Red Light, Green Light or Hide and Seek?

Here are my thoughts:

This chapters radio best of 'Tom Matts Boomers Rock' radio talk show features a well known physician Dr. Mathew Zatkin who graduated from Michigan State Universities College of Osteopathic Medicine in 2010. He completed his residency in Neuromusculoskeletal and Osteopathic Manipulative Medicine and is currently serving as faculty at MSU's OMM Clinic. If chronic pain has been an issue for you or someone you know this episode will shed some interesting takeaways, enjoy!

WEEK 24

Subject: Amazon Active

February 15

From: Tom Matt

To: Jeff Bezos

Hey Jeff,

As generations of people move through their lives, there are going to be certain behaviors that will carry-over. Some of those maturation lessons we learn, younger people don't think about much, but as you mature and see life through a different lens.

Here is this week's thought on inspiring and helping a generation toward self improvement. It is called, drum-roll please, wait, wait, wait:

'Amazon-Active'

Kinda catchy don't you think!

Today, everything is changed: Social Security and Medicare face deep problems, traditional pensions are almost obsolete, and the 2008 financial meltdown is still relatively fresh and frightful for many and interest rates on saving are pitiful.

So, what will we do to make growing older with dignity more attractive?

It is called "Walking through the front door of the ReFirement Zone" Boomers Rock style!

'Amazon-Active' is the golden ticket.

When I wrote 'Maximize Your Quality of Life' a few years ago I had a section that is the exercise/fitness section, however I changed my catch-phrase from exercise/fitness to 'activities that promote movement that are fun'. Middle Living and Superior Seniors do not, with the emphasis on NOT, want to be preached to.

We know we need to be more ACTIVE (catching the Amazon-Active theme here?) fitness, exercise, for the bulk of these 150 million or so people is for much younger generations.

Kinda like Airbnb, Lyft, Uber, Yerdly, and even BuzzFeed, not our proverbial cup of anything let alone tea.

By the way what's a 'Yerdly'?

A whole massive group wants trust, brand recognition, inspiration, teammates and the biggest of all SIMPLE!

'Amazon-Active' comes through the back door and kicks the crap out of all of the developers out there, it hits the sweetest of spots and it helps the people with two big things, desire for quality of life and money!

We Middle Living adults and Superior Seniors must invest in skills and stronger healthier bodies if we will remain employed, active, happier and self-reliant.

Research suggests that we remain in better health when we delay retirement.

And since we can remain better connected with friends and co-workers as well as remaining physically more active, generating a paycheck, and not dipping into our savings makes this whole concept appealing.

Eliminating the retirement mentality means that your money will last longer and keep growing, leaving you in better financial shape. Stay engaged, join 'Amazon-Active'.

Which by the way is an exclusive club tied to 'Prime-Membership,' see the past two weeks of idea submissions.

The trends are clearly here, and with a small amount of planning, inspiration and teamwork maximized QOL well past 90 is totally achievable. We must have a plan, and we must think 'transitional'.

Here is the good news.

We're living longer and, for the most part, healthier, than in the past. Both our mental and physical functioning in later life now exceeds that of our forefathers and foremothers. My own parents, born in 1937 and 1941 faced a life expectancy of somewhere in the neighborhood of 55-65 at birth. They are both still alive and doing great in their 70s. Surviving to age 70 was rare in my grandfather's era, now those days are long gone for us Middle Living (45-75) and Superior Seniors adults (76 and up).

I like to think that reaching the age of 80 will be viewed as "the new 50" with centenarians (age 100+), our fastest growing age group who are embracing the Boomers Rock mentality of the ReFirement Zone and 'Amazon-Active' works.

You just gotta keep it simple, and you need an example of how it works.

The end of retirement is already prompting a global reconsideration of how we think about the life cycle. For economic growth and greater security, we'll need to find new ways to work to 100+ while investing for the long haul in our health, mental faculties, friends, family, neighbors and society.

'Amazon-Active,' these ideas keep coming.

One of these days, Jeff, you and I will discuss how a Middle Living irreverent, avocational talk show host, author, personal trainer, dad, husband with a full time day job (who just won a Michigan Association of Broadcast 2014 award, imagine that), sent you a pile of ideas on how to change the world and we laughed about it how much fun we created!

Who cares about run on sentences when you are writing Jeff Bezos for god's sake!

Inspiration comes in many sources, you just need a driver for the bus!

Peace,

Tom

ps-
Since the last two replies have been from someone named Madhu I want to thank you Madhu for reading my ideas. I hope that in fact you do forward these thoughts and ideas on, because I would hate to think this is so much a form email back to a customer. At some point I would love to be able to say you were the one who did not pass judgement on these ideas and just let them die on the vine, you actually saw something, because very good things are happening here, and these ideas can help even the biggest stars!

WEEK 25

Subject: Amazon Active 2

February 23

From: Tom Matt

To: Jeff Bezos

Hey Jeff,

In a continuation of the brand new 'Amazon Active' I spoke about last week, which to remind everyone is a free service for 'Prime' members, the more thoughts I have to help the world.

Last week I spoke about 'Amazon Active' as "the golden ticket," with the multitude of activities that 'Active' (I shortened the tag, you get it by now I am sure) we now move into helping improve cognitive skills through technological assistance. Keeping your head in the game of life, this is where another of the 'Active' possibilities start to emerge.

According to Professors of Psychiatry from the University of California, San Francisco, how we age is determined by our daily behavior and the choices we make. There are a growing number of studies from around the world showing that aging is not just genetics, but it is how we live, and this is where 'Active' can provide options, opportunities, fun and collaboration.

As I stated last week, Middle Living, and Superior Seniors are, "a whole massive group wants trust, brand recognition, inspiration, teammates and the biggest of all SIMPLE!"

'Active' has an opportunity to be the platform, using integration of tech and family.

Deciding to live better is increasingly the same as living younger, the 'Active' platform does this.

How?

One way is integrating activities, a scorecard and brain games. The 'Active' playbook is simple yet elegant, appealing to the Middle Living/Superior Seniors as the target customer.

The integration of the Kindle Fire platform and smart phones gives us the golden ticket of technology and start the 'Active' tidal wave of enthusiasm. Listen to what Michael Scanlon, Chief Science officer of Lumosity has to say about their work, "our basic intention was to release a product that helps people improve cognitive abilities", and with revenues topping $1 Billion in 2012 and projections say $6 Billion by 2020 according to market research firm Sharp Brains the potential is unbelievable.

(Since the writing of this email Lumosity has had its issues. "Lumosity to Pay $2 Million to Settle FTC Deceptive Advertising Charges for Its "Brain Training" Program. Federal Trade Commission" Not to be a I told you so, but I will further on in this email. Mastering a video game is fine and dandy, but increasing brain health????? (http://1.usa.gov/1P41WP9)

Critics are howling, as they should. Before you get all revved up about spending time mastering a video game maybe you should look at the opportunity cost to the customer, the Middle Living/Superior Senior these games are targeting. Playing a video game does not make you smarter; it makes you a smarter game player. Let me be clear I love this tool in my 'Active' toolbox, I like the brain game platforms and they have their place. Everything comes down to balance; 'Active' helps us stay in proverbial homeostasis.

Finding the middle of this road is where 'Active' rides, we want to encourage our demographic in multiple ways. We use 'Active' and our scorecard platform to include healthy dietary choices, 'Active' points. Regular and consistent meditation, 'Active' point, learning new things, including licensed and approved games, 'Active' point and movement another 'Active' point, so I think you will see the point here!

Frankly the many ways we could gather points could be endless, it is all about being 'Active', being part of the family, and staying connected.

More next time, until then-

Peace,

Tom

WEEK 26

Subject: The Think Tank

March 1

From: Tom Matt

To: Jeff Bezos

Hey Jeff,

My mission statement for Boomers Rock Media is as follows:
"Boomers Rock inspires and educates audiences on ways to positively transform their lifestyles through application of our core values in radio, video, web based apps and literature."

When I received a Facebook message from Amazon Kindle Direct Publishing this week I had to think about the past couple of weeks and my letters to you about my thought of 'Amazon Active' and how your Kindle direct fits into the many different avenues that can improve the lives of millions of people.

The coaching that could be done, the inspiration that could be gleaned the stories that could be shared, you guys are barely scratching the surface of the most underutilized resource we now possess, the Middle Living and Superior Seniors.

And by the way, I love my Kindle Fire!

Yes, we have talked about this, and yes I continue to share my passions for the 150 million or so people in this demographic, call me crazy, but I cannot help it.

American Exceptionalism is not being an elitist, it is the abilities to change the world for the better. Just like some little outfit called Amazon, a game changer.

During the 20th century the population of the world increased from 1.6 billion to over 6 billion people. The only way we stayed ahead of the game is that technological advances allowed us to increase production. Technology, however, inevitably extracts its own toll on the Earth, so we cannot count on technology to save us forever. We have to use tech better, we need to encourage forward thinking, we need stories of survival, and overcoming adversity.

Living creatively, I kind of relate it to a big think tank, is an opportunity to mine gold from the millions of people who want to be included. What 'Amazon Active' does is encourage participation, it becomes the depository of ideas, and then shares them, via KDP.

What the world needs is inspiration and inclusiveness, the aging of the world should not be the slowing down of progress, it should be the accelerator. We lose an incredible amount of skill and experience when our system is constructed to a standard of life that disregards valuable human capital. With finite resources, time being the most precious, we recycle every everything from paper to plastic, but we send our most valuable of resource of human assets to wither away. The pinnacle of life is right in front of all of us but for some reason millions cannot see it.

KDP is just one small part of the Amazon think tank of potentials, 'Amazon Active' another of the ways to utilize and motivate. Having a think tank is better than anyone can imagine, and a heck of a lot more fun.

Peace,

Tom

WEEK 27

Subject: R-Squared

March 8

From: Tom Matt

To: Jeff Bezos

Hey Jeff,

In keeping with my goal of writing to you for a year, I would like to tell you that last week's edition was the half-way point. Yes that means 26 emails since I started my campaign to share ideas for changing the Middle Living/Superior Senior demographic, a culture change led by my favorite company Amazon.

Goals are achievable if you keep pushing the stone, stay focused and have passion, all of which you exhibited in building Amazon. It is something that needs to be encouraged and expressed more to make our country and people understand that dreams can come true.

Email 27, this one, is a short one, just a change-up, catch your breath and I hope some of my ideas may resonate with you. Creativity comes in many forms and from many places, when a big company thinks they know it all, than creative destruction is just around the corner.

Becoming a dominant solution takes guts, nimbleness, and a willingness to step up and inspire.

I call this R-Squared, 'Relentless-Resiliency'!

Peace,

Tom

WEEK 28

Subject: Amazon's Waterloo according to John Mackey

March 15

From: Tom Matt

To: Jeff Bezos

Hey Jeff,

I just finished reading an article titled "Whole Foods/ Half Off" written by Brad Stone in Bloomberg Businessweek, interesting article on the Whole Foods duo CEO's of John Mackey and Walter Robb. The story featured Mackey as the person of interest.

On February 1st in my weekly correspondence with you, I shared the idea of expanding your 'Prime Pantry' theme to perhaps include a hybrid of Amazon Prime, Prime Pantry and 'Aging in Place'. I introduced you to the Meals on Wheels folks, the 21st century version of how things may get done. I thought it was a great idea for my favorite company, Amazon, to really consider the aging population as a catalyst for not only changing the way older adults receive their essentials, but enabling a better quality of life for millions who need help.

I still think the idea has major potential.

Jeff, my boomer brother I have some bad news. Mr. Mackey stated in the above article that "the capital-intensive AmazonFresh foray into grocery delivery will be Amazon's 'Waterloo'."

And Brad Stone wrote the Amazon Store book.

Wow!

Dang, Jeff, I am still your pal and we haven't even met, yet. Speaking of that you realize you have an open invitation to the radio talk show, I can help you out since the 'Waterloo' is around the corner!

Maybe I am feeling a little bit giddy about receiving our first Michigan Association of Broadcast awards for excellence in broadcasting this past week, thank you, but when the world see's what the combination of giant Amazon and fledgling award winner Boomers Rock people are going to be shocked.

Waterloo, how about touchdown! It is all about helping people, not cutting them.

There is plenty of need in the world and no time for predictions of others demise.

As your grandfather said "it's harder to be kind than clever."

Peace,

Tom

8

RECOGNIZING MY CHOICES

"When we hate our enemies, we are giving them power over us: power over our sleep, our appetites, our blood pressure, our health, and our happiness."

Dale Carnegie

One of the best things that has happened in my life is understanding that 'Recognizing My Choices' holds the key to everything I want to change in my life. Recognizing that my personal self-improvement is completely predicated on retaining my personal power and choosing to 'reclaim' my life.

I am not going to be a victim of my own choices, I am not going to just give away my power. To continue my daily journey of self-improvement I need to:

Reframing how we perceive our lives can sometimes help us retain our personal powers. We can shift the perception just a very little bit and following these tips may help just a bit:

Peace

In keeping with the theme of presenting the best of 'Tom Matts Boomers Rock' radio talk show and sharing our diversified categories and experts this chapter it is jobs and work with AARP's best-selling author Kerry Hannon. This episode, like every one that Kerry has recorded with us is dynamite and you will not be disappointed.

WEEK 29

Subject: Inclusiveness

March 23

From: Tom Matt

To: Jeff Bezos

Hey Jeff,

Last night while watching the NCAA basketball tournament I saw an ad for Amazon Prime. I watched the next few ads that followed then I asked my wife Sandy to please rewind back to the Amazon ad of a minute and a half ago. Typically we fast forward through television ads, this time however I was rewinding to see what my favorite company was pitching.

Free two day shipping, music and movies. Flashy and clever, but it left me a little sad. Your people can do better, so much better.

It is not my point to be hypercritical, I am one of the loyalist of loyal and an advocate for everything you do, I have written about this to you many times. Amazon Prime is the conduit of enabling benefits and it can be so much more than two day shipping, music and movies, it can be the great enabler! It can be the breaker of barriers and the builder of communities; it can and should be 'AP-Squared'.

Michael Streger of Colorado State University has created a Laboratory for the study of Meaning and Quality of Life. His study, which he conducted with over 250,000 people, found that as far as the meaning in life it is the relationships that matter to humans more than anything else. That those relationships reinforce our sense of value, require us to engage, and ultimately help us grow, Amazon Prime Squared can be that great enabler, and inclusiveness builder, a mechanism to harness energy, a game changer!

Everyone wants to enjoy a happy, healthy life, filled with hopes of longevity and promise. We look for the trigger, the catalyst, the inclusive club, a place to plug into a diverse network of relationships that can form affections for anything and everything. Not an obligatory must do, an impassioned want to, so that new experimentation, new options, new products, and new friendships can be nurtured, it is what makes a good network great, and it is what makes a great service the best.

Amazon Prime Squared can be the leveler, the game changer, the service, the team builder, rally point and the great includer.

Join us and live longer, happier and smarter, sounds like a plan to me.

Peace.

Tom

THE THIRD REPLY!

03/24/2015

Amazon.com Executive Customer Relations <orders4@amazon.com>

Dear Thomas,

Thanks for being a loyal customer of Amazon and taking the time to write to us with your feedback about the benefits of prime. I can tell you've given this a lot of thought, and we're grateful you took the time and opportunity to send us your idea.

We are always happy to hear our customers' thoughts on how we can improve the services we offer. To ensure your idea is reviewed, I've shared your comments with our Prime team for their consideration when planning future improvements.

We're constantly fine-tuning our presentation to provide our customers with the greatest value, selection, and information for their online purchasing decisions.

However, we ask that all such proposals be submitted in writing to our corporate address:

Amazon.com
Attention: Marketing
P.O. Box 81226
Seattle, WA 98108-1226
USA

Appropriate departments will evaluate your proposal and contact you if we determine it fits within our marketing plans. We're not currently offering compensation for unsolicited business ideas.

Thomas, please feel free to continue to send us any suggestions for improvement as your opinion and participation is valuable to us.

Regards,

Jahnavi K.
Executive Customer Relations
Amazon.com
http://www.amazon.com

WEEK 30

Subject: Amazon Health

March 30

From: Tom Matt

To: Jeff Bezos

Hey Jeff,

Many of the ideas I have floated to you have involved adding features to 'Amazon Prime'. I am not sure why, maybe it is the inclusiveness, maybe it's because I like 'Prime' so much, it is the group that makes it special. It draws people into that togetherness, the team and the family.

If you believe that something will work, belief in performance, then performance directly influences belief and the goals that we will set, make sense? The beliefs we hold about our ability to stay healthy and necessarily stick with plans directly affect our positive results.

'Prime' can build the belief, you just gotta believe in the power of 'Prime' itself!

I propose building a feature into 'Prime' a complete members only treasury of knowledge that can be accessed by members, a holding area of personal information and solutions. Very simple solutions, user open sourced answers, interactive in its beauty, special by its membership, data based purchases, test results, conditions, one source for medications, food, supplements and easily retrievable and safe.

Health protection, wellness encouraged, lifestyle simplified, 'Amazon Health' provided by 'Prime'!

If we can bring water to the desert, think Bill and Melinda Gates, (nice objectives but not so much for our country and people, no offense to the Gates'), then why not support home and support Americans.

Our country needs creative disruption. We should be able to use the group inclusiveness to build a new system, no contraindications, no multiple EMR sites, if you belong to Amazon Health we got your information, supplies, and your life covered!

Potentials are fun to dream about! You will never inspire a team and create reinvention by making people afraid to express creative ideas.

Medical supplies, record storage, on time delivery, great services and value add. Sincere caring and trust, only the way that a 'Prime' member comes to expect. When you are spoiled by service you build solid habits, and those habits bring consistent growth.

Aging gracefully done the right way, with aggressive pursuit of solid lifestyle decisions.

Just another way to engage the masses and build brand loyalty while helping our country become a better place for all generations. Amazon Health, another kinda catchy thought.

Peace,

Tom

PS-
By the way I packaged and sent the whole set of 29 previous emails to your marketing address supplied to me last week. It looked pretty good for a rough draft, maybe someone will see it, maybe there is a disrupter in your house that has a sense of urgency.

WEEK 31

Subject: Becoming Exceptional

April 5

From: Tom Matt

To: Jeff Bezos

Dear Jeff,

To become exceptional takes courage, outliers are simply that, they are fearless. These are the people that can take the existing world on and make change happen, creative souls with the mindset of throwing caution to the wind.

We need this in the 21st century more than ever.

American Exceptionalism is the suggestion that the United States is different from other countries in that it has a specific world mission to spread liberty and democracy. It is not a notion that the United States is quantitatively better than other countries or that it has a superior culture, but rather that it is "qualitatively different".

If super successful companies and organizations can fall apart, when their models of operation in the past were so prosperous, then what happened? Is it that creativity became stifled and the challenges to look deep, think innovatively were not important anymore? Did they lose the energy and drive, become soft and forget that become supremely takes continual effort?

This was the mindset of the end of the 20th century and what our generation lived through.

Too often the Middle Living Superior Senior demographic has known no other way. When your DNA has been exposed to a certain beliefs and patterns you become a very limited thinker. On the radio show I use the analogy of a 30 or 40 year merry-go-round, you finally get off and have no idea what just happened.

Time to change that mentality, time to disrupt the status quo and time to encourage the new tribal behavior; it is only through education that we resurrect the exceptional talent of Middle Living adults.

Salmon Kahn created the Kahn Academy in 2006, and MOOC learning has made noise in education, but I am here to tell you as a Middle Living adult who spent nine years finishing my long dormant college career at Michigan State University, completing my Bachelors in 2006 and Masters in 2009 at 49 years old, those types of programs do not fit the 100 million or so people in the demographic I reach out to.

I hope that Boomers Rock can be a conduit of information from experts to end users. You first inspire with seeds of thought, and let people choose through a combination of delivery mechanisms, written, radio, web based, etc,,,,

The Middle Living Channel from Amazon is an idea whose time has come, an exclusive, a conduit that can work.

This is the value add to millions, the buy in to the Boomers Rock and Prime family, the diversified and ongoing learning that kicks the old habits out and brings new in. Finding that one place where the Middle Living can again become exceptional, where Superior Seniors can share their talent, Prime builds on the 'Ten-R Standards' which are:

Followed lastly by the Prime Directive-Reward; because it is through the rewards that behavior change sticks, that societal Exceptionalism blossoms and the tribe reunites to serve all. Inspire and educate, create and nurture, share and love, it is totally doable.

Exciting, for sure, exceptional, absolutely!

Peace,

Tom

THE FOURTH REPLY!

4/9/2015

Powers, Alice <apowers@amazon.com>

Dear Tom,

I hope you don't mind my responding on Jeff's behalf. Although he does read his email, his schedule doesn't always allow him to respond personally.

I wanted to get back to you to let you know that I've taken the liberty of forwarding your information on to our Business Development department. Jeff has empowered talented people on this team to work closely with and make strategic decisions about these issues. I feel confident entrusting your inquiry to them.

If your idea would contribute significantly and directly to our business goals you will be contacted. Thanks for thinking of us.

Kind regards,
Alice Powers

WEEK 32

Subject: Fun

April 12

From: Tom Matt

To: Jeff Bezos

Hey Jeff,

Today is my dad's birthday, he is 77 years old, and as idiosyncratic as he is, his love for life never wavered. For many, loving life is non-existent.

Time to change the narrative to this story!

In his book Flourish Dr. Martin Seligman argues that happiness is too narrow a concept, sometimes I believe that it is too broad, but hey I like Dr. Seligman's idea a lot. He stated that happiness is a mood and is quite fleeting, and in the whole scope of life we should be focusing on a different goal. That is well-being.

I like it, a ton!

Dr. Seligman broke it down to five core components:

Influencing a generation or two, Middle Living/Superior Seniors, takes the awakening of wisdom and experiences. We can create a much larger culture shift by mining and encouraging the sharing of those stories and accomplishments, all 100 million plus of them.

Jeff, our job is to encourage the freedom and inspire our brothers and sisters to remember fun. The great paradigm shift is awaiting the catalyst.

Cognitive dissonance runs rampant in the Middle Living/Superior Senior demographics because we have too much information; things have gotten way too complicated. We do not need more facts, we need help finding our embedded stories and memories, the tribe needs a leader to step up and inspire.

People make bad decisions, I know I did, not because we do not have the information or the facts, it is because we ignore the facts or do not think they are important enough or apply to us, why? Because we fall into this thing called life, and we lose sight of fun, we forget, and we take the easiest way to the end of our day, the habit.

It is Alice's rabbit hole.

The stories of millions will illustrate that we are not alone in the confusion, and the perception that life sucks is just that, a perception, certainly not a fact.

That is cognitive dissonance at its psychological finest!

Jeff you are all about empowerment, what Amazon does is lead to new thoughts.

It has for me and it can for the millions who are lost. Life is not hard and does not suck; it is the perception behind the belief that leads to the interpretation.

Changing that interpretation, that is our goal.

Fun does not mean trouble, or sin or rabble rousing; it means "experiential explosiveness"!

Life is beautiful and fun, well-being is directly proportional to the five core competencies. It is about igniting lives, stories, memories, and empowerment.

I have multiple categories on the radio talk show because I want to hear the stories from the experts.

People need what we provide, remember last week I proposed the Amazon Middle Living channel; it is all about the conduit of good information.

100 million or more people thirst for this, time to quench the craving, time to help the masses.

Peace,

Tom

9

FANTASTIC FIVE PERCENT

"My grandmother started walking five miles a day when she was sixty. She's ninety-seven now, and we don't know where the hell she is".
Ellen DeGeneres

There is a new trend I have been noticing recently and I like it. I like it A LOT!

It is called the "Active Workstations" and it is assisting all of us achieve what I call the 'Fantastic 5 Percent'.

FFP (Fantastic Five Percent) works this way. I give you 8 hours to work and 8 hours to sleep, this leaves us with 8 hours to use however we want. 5% of those 8 hours equates to 24 minutes, all I am suggesting is taking one minute each working hour (8 minutes) and stand up for one minute while at work. Doing this gives us a jump start on our FFP for the day. Now we only having 16 minutes left, you decide whatever movement you want to do. Active workstations are awesome because you get your FFP in plus some. However for those of us who don't have the "active workstation" luxury don't fret because those last sixteen minutes are a piece of cake, it is just having the target in mind to achieve our goal.

The entire modern world is constructed to keep us sitting down. When we drive, we sit. When we work at an office, we sit, when we watch TV, we sit. The time has come to use your FFP goal to eliminate just SOME of the sitting. Yes, standing counts, watching TV standing up counts, walking up stairs counts, it all adds up! Remember just 16 more minutes!

Prolonged sitting, meaning sitting for eight to 12 hours or more a day, increases your risk of developing type 2 diabetes by 90%.
http://bit.ly/1SQsadL
Say what!

The FFP gives us a target, it is simple, those that are blessed with "active workstations" halleluiah, those of us who are not so lucky, fear not because simplicity is in our corner.

Some other FFP suggestions:

Peace

This chapter and its best of broadcast of 'Tom Matts Boomers Rock' radio talk show is titled, "A Bold New Approach to Addiction and Recovery". Author Erica Spiegelman, 'Rewired', is dynamite in our discussion of substance abuse, recovery, and deep profound caring. This episode will open your eyes to an issue that has the potential to destroy lives, families and relationships.

WEEK 33

Subject: The Faith Generator Mentality

April 19

From: Tom Matt

To: Jeff Bezos

Hey Jeff,

Have you ever wondered what if Bob Metcalfe had never conceived of his 'law'? (Bob Metcalfe is an internet pioneer who devised value of a telecommunications network is proportional to the square of the number of connected users of the system ($n2$). For example the proliferation of the fax machine.)

What if he had decided that instead of being a forward thinker and pioneer he decided to forgo his thoughts on the number of users in a network and their value to that said network, and instead opened a Burger King.

Would the world be a better place?

If Henry Ford had not listened to his wife and got over his insecurities and followed through with his dreams, would he have wound up an electrician instead of an industrial pioneer, would the world be the same?

What if you, Jeff, had decided that buying books online was never possible, and instead your dream became franchising the Bezos' Detailing & Car Wash dynasty? Would that have been the path for your success? Because we all know that you are a stickler for details, and of course everyone can use a good detailer!

Would the world be a better place?

Boldness take guts, creativity takes dreaming, expanding your personal horizons takes determination.

You gotta feel the urge to be different, you gotta be more than you, and it is all about unlimited potential and not fitting in. You just gotta be different, you gotta believe.

The Amazon Faith Generator Mentality has arrived!

Self-improvement begins the very first thing in the morning when you open your eyes, when you have the burning belief and faith that change is doable, that you are part of a team and a connected purpose; now you have what the Amazon Faith Generator Mentality is powered by.

Too many of us become locked in, being the same and not making noise or a difference. We need that thing to be a part of. We need the Amazon Faith Generator Mentality can do and that is to unlock our doubts, to enable, to build confidence, to give us our connection.

We need a cause!

Remember the Yuppies, or the Hippies, or the 99%? What made the Civil Rights, Women's Rights, Equal Rights movements roar? What makes a zealot, or a crusader; what creates a movement? It is the non-conformist, the radical who believes that influencing a generation is doable, even if they do have a lot of miles on their tires. It will be the Amazon Faith Generator Mentality; the trusted source, the rallying point, the go to, the Godfather!

Become irreplaceable, be the one, create undying love and you have something special.

There is the connection economy, the purpose economy, the digital economy, the consumer economy, what we need is the inspiration economy. The common theme in our world is it is all about the people; the inspiration economy works for me, because without relationships and conviction our tanks are empty and we have nothing.

Generate faith and you have something!

Everything we do matters, our duty is to help others see past the negativity, our duty is beautiful and empowering, our duty is to provide hope and our duty is to lead by example.

If I didn't want to be great then I should never have started my company. As a conduit of information to inspire and educate we have tremendous upside, and we have what matters, FAITH!

Remember your vision Jeff my man, you had faith and envisioned a company that makes money by delivering value to rather than extracting from your customers, that took inspiration, that took balls and that took faith.

Generating Faith, not an idea that a conformist will think of, sitting on the sideline is not in my being, and I don't believe it is yours either. Until next week,

Peace,

Tom

WEEK 34

Subject: The Bucket List

April 26

From: Tom Matt

To: Jeff Bezos

Hey Jeff,

In the movie 'The Bucket List,' Billionaire Edward Cole (Jack Nicholson) and car mechanic Carter Chambers (Morgan Freeman) are total strangers, until destiny lands them in the same hospital room. If you mention destiny to my almost 19 year old daughter she will cringe with disdain, must be a GenY thing. (Together Jack Nicholson and Morgan Freeman illustrate the 'potential of the 'Odd Couple' and how they change each others lives.

We have a chance to inspire and motivate millions by developing our symbiotic relationships. Or would it be synergistic, whichever, opportunity to change a generation, the country and the world, well I know you have done it once or twice.

Experienced mentors rock the world, that is why I am now at email 34 to you! At some point the hope is that through your generosity and helping another you will illustrate the power of outreach.

This week I began working toward a long term dream, this one will take some time and lots of practice: playing the drums!

Yes, this took convincing the wife that the banging won't drive her insane, and yes, I have a private tutor, and yes, I bought a used drum set. You improve your brain by trying and learning new things, here we go again.

Like the 'Miracle on 34th Street' film I went to my favorite store, Amazon, gathered information on drums, looked around the Internet and I found my price point. No, I did not buy from Amazon, like Kris

Kringle in the movie I took the advice and went to another source, (Craigslist), but the point is I trusted Amazon enough that I first went to you to do my research. It was then that I knew I was getting the value add that helped me convince the blonde bookkeeper, Sandy my wife.

Oh, and buying on eBay, I have bought one thing there and that is probably it. It is not the Amazon experience that is for sure. And yes, they have used drum sets, but there was no way I was going to drive to Nebraska to pick up a deal!

Trust in Amazon is the linchpin to many more purchases, references and referrals.

What I do with my radio show is share the energy and story of never giving up, trying those new things, experimenting, and coming to terms with the fact that aging is actually cool. It is our desire to fulfill dreams that makes you the Kris Kringle and me the messenger.

Challenges are good, and having a source that makes you feel secure in everything you do has unlimited potential. Last week I mentioned the 'Faith Generator', that is what it is, and it may sound kind of corny, but in the end if people use your services to reinforce their dreams isn't that a really cool thing?

When Morgan Freeman and Jack Nicholson became the oddest of couple, magic occurred. Mountains were climbed, race cars driven. I now have my drums to practice with, next Spanish, and then maybe another body-building show when I am 60; it is the examples of ordinary doing the extraordinary that make the story.

Oh and a nationally syndicated radio talk show, best-selling books, a television show and network, and lastly, working with you, it's all good and getting better every day. That is all we can do, inspire greatness.

Without the dreams you can never achieve, right Kris Kringle!?

Peace,

Tom

WEEK 35

Subject: Amazon Entourage

May 4

From: Tom Matt

To: Jeff Bezos

Hey Jeff,

Recently I saw an ad on television for something called, Trivago. It is a website that compares websites for hotels, it was well done and informational, but it misses our sweet spot entirely! They claim the average American will visit seven different websites before booking a hotel, they claim to compare 150 websites for value, hmmmm, for example-
And on and on and on and on, do you see a problem here?
On the Boomers Rock Radio Talk Show, I specifically chose travel as a category because I know that the Middle Living/Superior Senior, demographic spends more, travels more, has more multigenerational travel plans and is the sweetest of sweet spots. I also know that too much information, too many choices, and not enough trust is our newest opportunity to owning the this market in several ways.
I have a code name for it, Amazon Entourage, and building this members only group fits really nicely into Amazon Prime. Follow this line of thinking for a second:
Amazon Entourage has several layers that will take the complexities and overwhelming data and boil it down. This service will encourage people share their stories, it is our own family of references. It builds on what Amazon pioneered with its reviews and expands on it. It is a rating system, driven by end users for end users, sorted, rated, and quantified to make it easy to search.

And that is just the beginning; because from the reviews you can not only have the stories of real families building memories, but you are building a new community.

Ask someone what they got for their birthday last year and you get that blank look, but ask them where their family went on vacation the last time, and that might be 5 years ago, and they will remember instantly.

Multigenerational memories drive the train, and we fuel the engine.

The Boomers Rock radio talk show shares stories now, the Amazon Active television channel can share adventures (multiple shows, different genres) with the family adventure travel show as one of its leading programs.

Advertisers are pre-screened with targeted advertising and web based viewer analytics which Amazon has carefully researched. Advertisers also must meet a high level of integrity just to qualify to be allowed the right to this virgin demographic. If they (advertisers) are not reputable they don't get in, another layer of protection and tremendous credibility builder for the members.

Pitching a trip, adventure vacation, or cruise to our demographics means multigenerational gold. With Amazon Entourage you can read about it, hear about it, and see it. Plus we encourage sharing it

Ding-Fricking-Ding!

It is a content driven world where we have the families, their stories, the experts, the value, radio and the television programming all wrapped up in one package, and the kicker is, you must be a Prime Member to partake in our travel club.

Amazon Entourage is exclusively for the Middle Living/Superior Senior market; it takes the tech mystery out and simplifies the entire process.

And the added value add of all of the exclusive stories to share!

Reality content at its finest, because it truly is REAL.

(Imagine that a reality television show that is actually real, novel concept and brilliant!)

When we select the best stories to share on radio and television it is content made in heaven, and families will love it. Advertisers will run to it and customers will flock to it. End users will want their stories out there, it is the sharing economy at its finest.

Lastly Jeff, this is just one of eight categories I share on the radio talk show.

The model works and this is just the tip of the entertainment, educational, inspirational, motivational iceberg. Helping people with good content, simplifying the game.

How come nobody else is doing this?

Peace,

Tom

WEEK 36

Subject: Amazing-Amazon-Adaptability (A-Cubed)

May 10

From: Tom Matt

To: Jeff Bezos

Hey Jeff,

Self-improvement is a journey that begins every day. It is never ending and it is a process that with the right mindset and tools can give people a magical gift, self-fulfillment, happiness and self-worth.

Abraham Maslow would say 'self-actualization,' the top of man's hierarchy of needs pyramid.

It is through self-improvement that every family, organization, and workplace can see incremental development which leads to efficiencies and profitability. There is only one way to the top of the pyramid, it is A-Cubed!

I have my top ten list to share with you that can lead us to the promised land. I first derived this list for my 'Maximize' book, chapter 16; this is the condensed Amazon version.

Short and sweet, because each of the ten points listed should be read, memorized, and adapted. Start with just one, remember incremental, and then build better people.

When all ten are adapted, then magic can occur, and the universe opens its potential to greatness!

Amazing-Amazon-Adaptability, (A-cubed), is sharing your success, which makes your life the best that it can be. Post this top-ten list on every wall in your many facilities to remind people that you care and watch the change in production.

Need someone to share a story and fire up the troops, I am your guy!

Peace,

Tom

10

GENERATIONAL LEADERSHIP

In the book 'Sacred Hoops' Phil Jackson writes, "creating a successful team...is essentially a spiritual act. It requires the individuals involved to surrender their self-interest for the greater good so the whole adds up to more than the sum of its parts."

I am learning, through the blessing of interviewing very smart people on the radio show, that the most successful people are always the most reflective and giving. That becoming a self-reflective person requires an individual to surrender the 'I' mentality and live the 'We' lifestyle. Self reflection leads to self-improvement and incremental change.

I love this, and want to become better at it!

To make a positive change in others' lives I must focus on the community, the younger generations and communicate that desire by sharing my own positivity toward life. There is no other way!

My great friend Dr. Debbie Heiser, a psychologist from New York and regular on the radio program, calls it 'Generativity', where the mindset becomes guiding the next generation toward self-improvement through optimism and experience sharing. I can begin each day with the thought of providing better service, outlooks, happiness, vision and lead by example. In essence, make a difference in others' lives so they can pull from my positive energy and share it with others.

When the positive energy is abundant, optimism is boundless. I am smiling and cheerful and eyes are alive with the juice of life, the potential for Generativity is unlimited. Using my experience as a Middle Living adult is all about teaching and leading, sharing the experiences that I have lived through so that others can have a better life.

We all can improve the world by:

Peace

This chapters best of 'Tom Matts Boomers Rock radio talk show features a dynamic show titled "Building more 'Communities for a Lifetime' in Michigan: Enhancing Economic Development" with guest Brigit Hassig. In this episode you can hear of how ideas can transform lives and communities, moving past the 20th century retirement mindset.

WEEK 37

Subject: Will the Apple Watch Save Your Life

May 17

From: Tom Matt

To: Jeff Bezos

Hey Jeff,

In this month's Men's Fitness magazine (May, 2015) there is a really great article on the Apple watch, titled "Will the Apple Watch Save Your Life".

It features such headings as-

We know there is no such thing as a silver bullet, but poaching talent by the truck load, well it may work. Many of the features noted in the article are spot on with worthiness, heart rate monitoring, for example is critical and useful, I have used a Polar for years and it works great and is very helpful in monitoring your level of workouts.

I am in the minority of Middle Living/Superior Senior adults who use these, and therein lay the problem.

Generationally gadgets are not worth diddly if you do not use them; information and advice, collaboration, and sharing what does work is the silver bullet. I wrote about a similar note to you and how we could utilize tech on September 28th, 2014. "How can smartphones, portable devices change the practice of medicine", teaching and helping the world to embrace the compelling 'why' and 'how' is the quest.

In the above article it talked about how Credit Suisse "recently estimated that up to 40% of our health-care costs are directly related to overconsumption of sugar and the havoc it wreaks on our bodies."

One of the chief goals of the 'Apple Manhattan Project' is a non-invasive glucose monitor for future generations of the Apple watch, best of luck with that one!

According to the article "John Smith, the former chief scientific officer of Johnson & Johnson's LifeScan, has spent decades on it (glucose monitoring) and chronicled his journey in a book called Hunting the Deceitful Turkey." He wrote that "in 30-plus years, more than 100 research groups have spent hundreds of millions of dollars trying to create a glucose monitor, yet not one has managed to get a single product to market."

Yikes!

How about informing people that eating less white bread and weaning ourselves off of soda could instantly improve glucose and that could happen today, my 'Fantastic-Five' percent plan could be implemented with no effort at all, make a massive difference and change that 40% number overnight.

(If you would like a more detailed explanation of my 'Fantastic-Five' just let me know)

Yes, glucose monitoring is noble, and blood sugar is something everyone needs to appreciate. What we need is consistent information monitoring, like I talked about in my email from December 7th titled the 'Linus Project'. I talked about coordination and protection of information. This is all the over 100 million Middle Living/Superior Seniors need. They need to have a place that they can trust, a team of like-minded souls, a tribe of the heart.

It is 'Back to the Future' at its finest, where communication among a family is strong and knowledge is shared. It is quality services that can be implemented quickly, the suite of such which fall under the 'Amazon-Active' umbrella. Open the 'Amazon-Active' umbrella, and watch what can happen.

Membership driven, fraternity-like in its loyalty, inclusiveness at its finest, the 'Active' family will dominate. Thirty years and hundreds of millions of dollars? No way, we need solutions now.

I love gadgets, but I love the family more.

Peace,

Tom

WEEK 38

Subject: Practicing Empathy

May 25

From: Tom Matt

To: Jeff Bezos

Hey Jeff,

Last week I had an occasion to attend an event in Appleton, Wisconsin hosted by the bank BMO Harris. The topic of the event was 'Living to 100', most of the guests were investors with the bank, the bank hosts these events as a thank you to their clients, and the rest of the attendees were employees of the bank. Their term for the small teams is 'Premier Bankers,' two person teams of bankers and financial advisors.

I had an opportunity to sit with two of these employees (both Gen Y), and it was enlightening.

There is a growing body of work, Jeff, that shows that empathy is essential for building meaningful and trusting relationships, something that we all need, especially the Middle Living/Superior Senior demographic.

It has been shown that empathy is related closely to professional and academic success, my sitting with these two thirty-something bankers at an event to coach people to understand how to live to 100 is a perfect example of how large the generational gap can be.

Empathy awareness can reduce prejudice and ill fitted values, we can use this to help our programming and services enhancing and building that lasting customer relational trust.

Teresa Wiseman, a nursing scholar in England identified four defining attributes of empathy; these can be used to engage the building of trust and understanding between generations.

1. To see the world as others see it
2. To be non-judgmental
3. To understand another person's feelings, and
4. To be able to communicate your understanding of that person's feelings

In order for a person to be empathetic, for example the two younger bankers I sat with, we must understand and be willing to recognize their perspective through THEIR lens. To be able to hear what the other person is saying, what they desire, what they want. In our world we sometimes focus on seeing the world through our own view, not the bigger view of the entire world.

The effectiveness of multi-generational coaching is dependent on developing empathetic skills. It takes, like any other acquired skill, deep practice. Becoming aware of the need to practice a behavior, compassion, empathy, understanding, or listening, is critical. It is the stories that can change perspectives and help the practice become efficient.

Efficient practice is a change agent, it is the key to our relational 21st century, becoming aware and seeing people through the different lens can change the world for the better.

The two bankers I sat with listened intently as I shared my story and values; they became more aware to the needs of their customers through our conversation. I believe they came away with a deeper understanding of the needs of older adults. Practicing empathy is a great tool for success in life and business. (It was interesting to me how little the younger Millennial bankers really knew about collaboration between the generations.)

The Prime Directive I have mentioned in earlier messages to you encompasses many opportunities to empower customers, employees, coaching them up. The Prime Directive inspires the desire to practice empathy. From the 'Middle Living Channel' to 'Amazon Active', the 'Ten R's Standard', or 'Prime-Fresh', etc. it is stories that can engage, it is the outstanding services that share the value of and depth in an empathetic organization.

Attitude puts you over the top, actions follow the rule. As Pema Chadron wrote,

"Compassion becomes real when we recognize our shared humanity."

Set the bar low enough and anyone can fall over, we will set the bar high by building better attitudes behaviors and beliefs.

Empathy, it does a body good!

Peace,

Tom

WEEK 39

Subject: Through Adversity Grows Opportunity

May 31

From: Tom Matt

To: Jeff Bezos

Hey Jeff,

So once again I find myself writing about an article that derides slams and/or harpoons my pals at Amazon, this of course means that I, like Perry Mason, must have a rebuttal. The article in question was forwarded to me from my brother.

Titled 'Worse than Wal-Mart: Amazon's sick brutality and secret history of ruthlessly intimidating workers,' excerpted from the book by Simon Head "Mindless: Why Smarter Machines Are Making Dumber Humans," 2014, Basic Books.

The subtitle to this article was "You might find your Prime membership morally indefensible after reading these stories about worker mistreatment."

Frankly, Jeff, 'thems-fightin' words in my world!

I know that flashy headlines sell, but man, Jeff can the author lighten up a little and grow a pair of perspectives, geez.

He wrote, "Jeff Bezos, Amazon's founder and CEO, came in second in the Harvard Business Review's 2012 world rankings of admired CEO's and Amazon was third in the CNN's 2012 list of the world's most admired companies," sweet!

Hold on, the torpedo had just been launched!

The article goes on to borderline slander (strictly my opinion) Amazon and its treatment of employees in Europe, and how really, really badly they are treated, tracked, monitored and your 'hegemonic' way (Simon's word) rules the roost.

My response to all of this I can quantify with a big fat, "So what"!

I mean really, there are so many other issues in the world that are so much more relevant to the human condition. And these are 'jobs' right, no one forces you to take a job. A successful employer having rules, my gosh the blasphemy!

Here is a stat that really makes me want to cry and something I am hoping we can work together to try and fix, (the purpose of writing you every week for a year), try this one on for size.

"Despite a rising economy since the beginning of the 1990's, U.S. personal bankruptcy filings tripled- from approximately 750,000 in 1990 to 2,000,000 in 2005-with much of the increase resulting from family medical catastrophes. One million middle and upper-class U.S. families are forced into bankruptcy every year by the sickness industry."

I excerpted that quote from the new 'Wellness Revolution' by Paul Zane Pilzer, and it is a very clear example a truly serious issue, that we can, by working together , help resolve, solve and change the world for the better. Hegemony to the rescue!

'Through adversity grows opportunity'.

Making me think about my 'morally indefensible Prime Membership' is tantamount to deep inspiration and changing the world for the better. I cannot help if someone fills out an application to work for Amazon, receives a job and then God forgive a paycheck and benefits, that is a personal choice issue. What I can do is talk about helping and inspiring others through my own radio program, articles, books, stories, TV, emails, and build a movement that changes the world. I also can write you letters and inspire you to take a chance on something new.

My 'Personal-Prime' , like the idea of a 'Prime Directive', which I have shared with you, is a conduit to helping change the world for the better. I am glad we have such a conduit of great information (Amazon) because without it there is no radio program, books, articles and content that I personally have created.

So Mr. Simon, lighten up will ya!

Letter 39 in the bank, thirteen more to go and then we pull it together in the book. "How Amazon Changed a Generation, and Saved the World". I cannot wait to see how this whole thing ends because one thing I do have is faith and positive vibes that we are doing the right thing. The other big tech giants never saw this coming, they will wonder what happened when all of this is blows up!

Don't mess with my Prime, ever!

Peace

Tom

WEEK 40

Subject: Hillbilly Hand Fishin'

June 7

From: Tom Matt

To: Jeff Bezos

Hey Jeff,

I have to tell you some of the television content that is being created is ranging in scope from outstandingly brilliant to absurdly brilliant. I am not even sure that sentence makes any sense as I read it, please bear with me.

If I think in my Middle Living brain that 'Duck Dynasty' is the least funny, most ridiculous show ever and my GenY daughter and her husband think it is hilarious and the funniest thing ever, is it absurdly brilliant content?

Well I guess you could say 'for sure, because it's a hit' to that one since it is all about making people want to watch and become pretty much obsessed with the show.

I still do not get the whole thing, 'Duck-Callers'?

When I first saw my wife and daughters watching 'Say Yes to the Dress' it was almost intoxicating to me, it lulls you into the story, absurdity notwithstanding, brilliance taken to the depth of 'Bridezilla', another unfortunate family (my girls') favorite.

'Hillbilly Handfishin', 'Honey Boo-Boo', 'Moonshine', 'Swamp People', have all traditional TV execs come to the conclusion that what the American public wants is a mix of goofy and contrived "reality" shows and programming that showcases the ignorance of white southern rednecks?

It appears that you can and that this is the only demographic that it is still possible to belittle and make fun of without arousing widespread scandal.

Jed Clampett would be incensed, not to mention Granny or Jethro Bodine.

I need to talk to your guy Roy Price!

I read about Roy in Wired magazine, the 'original face-off' with Netflix's own Cindy Holland and how Netflix is dumping $300 million into their original programming budget while my pals over at Amazon are investing a mere $100 million.

Time for the sneak attack on Netflix, and all of these other content creators.

Roy and I need to talk.

If the Wired article is correct and Roy is looking for, and I quote, "a group of people for which this could be a favorite show" and "watching television is going to be more tailored to you" boy do I have some ideas on the demographic, the target audience, content and brainstorming. Roy is absolutely correct in his statement that "everything inconvenient or annoying about it (programming) will be innovated away" he is spot on.

Heck like most busy people with a career, vocation, dreams, and hobbies, I can speak directly about this, it's true!

Haven't I already sent you something on this recently, i.e. the Middle Living channel brought directly to you via the 'Prime Directive'?

Don't over think this one Jeff. Sometimes the 'David and Goliath collaboration can seriously bring home the counter to 'Redneck Millionaires'!

I mean really, has the vast majority of television viewers really sunk to this lowest common denominator. I do not think so.

Please have Roy send me a note, we got some catfish to fry and some moonshine to brew!

Peace

Tom

11

PUTTING 'FUN_CTION' INTO YOUR LIFE

"We came here with an idea that we were going to have to weather the storm or be the storm".

Mark Dantonio

Insist on being a hero, and then be one.

For a Middle Living or Superior Senior adult "function" may mean the capacity to carry groceries or get out of the bathtub, play on the floor with your grandchildren or even coach their athletic teams. Functional fitness and living with a positive sense of well-being is a goal that everyone should aim to achieve, giving ourselves the opportunity to live life to its optimum.

As our population is becoming "grayer," there is a growing need to stay engaged, not giving into stereotypical beliefs that as we get older we slow down. This is where the great challenge and the opportunity arises for us to lead by example. Running with our grandchildren is not out of the question, shooting hoops in the driveway isn't either.

For this reason, there has become a great need to educate active older adults to exercise safely and effectively so that their quality of life remains stronger and long-lasting. Group activities that are led by trained experts, personal trainer or coach offers a tremendous professional, social and economic opportunity. I encourage those of us looking for that 'next' thing to consider a transitional career as a group fitness instructor or certified trainer.

A Senior/Functional Fitness Specialist is a fitness professional who works with a cross section of different clients and is able to personalize their training program to help them meet a widely divergent variety of needs, with the understanding that "function" means different things to different people.

Staying in the game of life is our goal, putting the fun back into fun_ction is the plan, do your due diligence and love yourself more, it will make a world of difference.

Peace

In this chapters best of 'Tom Matt's Boomers Rock' radio talk show the emphasis is on technology and our health. Featuring author, speaker and expert entrepreneur Robin Farmanfarmaian this is a great episode to get a primer on what technology is doing and what we can expect in the future.

WEEK 41

Subject: Self-Efficacy and Your Resilience Muscle

June 14

From: Tom Matt

To: Jeff Bezos

Hey Jeff,

Self-efficacy is a term that really holds a lot of potential for the maturation of our country and the whole world. According to Albert Bandura, noted Psychologist and professor at Stanford, defines it as "the belief in one's capabilities to organize and execute the courses of action required to manage prospective situations." Dr. Bandura's work is widely found in many of the books I have read.

It is really great work, cutting edge stuff, and if we (multi-generationally) are trying to get a grip on living to 100 with quality of life, as I like to say all the time on the radio program, then 'self-efficacy' is a key term to understand.

It is through self-efficacy that you have the self-confidence to do what you do and achieve goals. How you feel you can execute your plan, and how successful you will be is self-efficacy.

Toss in resilience and then understanding the power of the combination, both resiliency and self-efficacy, and you have a major double-dip ice cream cone of supreme magnitude.

A great quote by Dr. Bandura illustrates what I am referring to:

"In order to succeed, people need a sense of self-efficacy, (basically self-confidence) to struggle together with resilience to meet the inevitable obstacles and inequities in life."

Build your 'resilience muscle' and watch your lift off to greatness soar! Giving a road map to new adventures builds a better world, here are some thoughts.

Some of the largest energy draining activities that lead to stressful lives is lacking self-confidence, negative media, and sitting around. People need to have that positivity and group connectedness to drive change. People need to know that greatness is a self-imposed inherent quality that everyone possesses, you just gotta find your own compelling 'why'.

Your resilience muscle needs to be trained, your self-confidence encouraged leading to a stronger sense of self-efficacy.

When you find those people who are successful, write them letters seek their mentorship and build that dynamic relationship because frankly you cannot have too many good people in your life.

Meeting the inevitable inequities in life, as Professor Bandura stated, is a journey. It is a mission and it is fun. It is all about giving yourself the best odds you can, and believing in being part of greatness and building a better planet.

Everyone wants to be on a winning team, because winners are special.

The 'Prime –Directive' is all about passion, health, connectedness, great coaching and of course winning!

Peace,

Tom

WEEK 42

Subject: It's Not the What, It's the How! (Chapter 1)

June 21

From: Tom Matt

To: Jeff Bezos

Hey Jeff,

Recently, I read an article in Fortune magazine called, 'The War on Big Food' by Beth Kowitt, the Trillion dollar food fight has just begun and it will not be the big boys/girls who win this war.

Back in March, letter 28, I wrote you and it was titled, 'Amazon's Waterloo according to John Mackey'. It was based on "Whole Foods/ Half Off" article written by Brad Stone in Bloomberg Business week. Just to refresh your memory of a pretty cocky statement by Mr. Mackey, "the capital-intensive AmazonFresh foray into grocery delivery will be Amazon's 'Waterloo'."

Mr. Mackey should worry more about the new mindset that Whole Foods is now being referred to as 'Whole Paycheck', and after reading the Beth Kowitt article all of the big players are sweating bullets in their $600.00 warmups. Is everyone in the world looking for a silver bullet?

It appears to me that they are, yes!

When an executive like Denise Morrison of Campbell's makes a statement that she has to "shift the center of gravity at Campbell's," Einstein's theory may be reworked. According to the article Ms. Morrison is in culture-paradigm shift mode by changing the essence and vocabulary of a company that started in 1869. They no longer 'process and manufacture' but they 'cook' and 'preserve' and employees follow 'recipes', not 'formulas'.

Hmmmmmmmmmmmmmmmmmm!

According to Ms. Kowitt's article 'Americans are willing to give up a lot for their newfound interest in wellness' and another quote by Paul Grimwood, Nestle's head of U.S. business, "in food, change is happening at a pace we've probably never seen before" and the willingness of people to alter and adopt new food trends "is at its highest level, probably ever!"

Double Hmmmmmmmmmmmmm!

Memo to Mr. Mackey, Ms. Morrison,and Mr. Grimwood:

It's Not the What, It's the How!

Jeff, recall that one of my favorite lines from the radio program is "through adversity grows opportunity," this issue with food is not that complicated, and it is not going to change with a new vocabulary, it all comes down to these things:

You can give people better labels, organic, non-processed, whole, fresh, and change your perceived stodgy 146 year old culture (Campbell's), but none of it matters. Campbell's, Nestle, Kellogg, General Mills can buy up all of the small guys they want, spend billions and over think this issue with meetings upon meetings with really, really smart people. The bottom line however is this:

It's Not the What, It's the How!

Through adversity grows opportunity.

Have ever heard of the 'Prime-Directive'?

No, you will!

Peace,

Tom

WEEK 43

Subject: It's not the What It's the How (Chapter 2)

June 28

From: Tom Matt

To: Jeff Bezos

Hey Jeff,

So last week we touched on the 'Big-Food' mindshift, panic, or cultural revolution in their ever changing paradigm. These examples are a mirror to all of the change that is occurring in the 21st century, especially in my sweet spot of the Middle Living/Superior Senior narrowcast.

First, a quick reminder for the business developers at Amazon, your people, the advisors Alice mentioned, you know, those super smart empowered people that are going to change the world:

As Baby Boomers transform concepts of growing older, they bring massive potential for businesses that target services and products for the even larger demographic of Middle Living/Superior Seniors. Remember you business development folks at Amazon, we are talking anyone age 45 and up. If there are 78 million boomers then the math is easy, it's a big number!

The overarching umbrella that is and will grow larger is of course Amazon's 'Prime-Directive'.

Remember in last week's letter I discussed big foods Trillion dollar issue, and how rebranding, reidentifying, and reformulating is nothing more than a lot of regurgitating? Campbell's Tomato soup (The 'What') is awesome, the complimentary grilled cheese along with it is tremendous, and is beautiful comfort food.

However, eating it several times a week (The 'How') is the issue.

We need more education, balance, and guidance and it is called the APD (Amazon Prime-Directive)

As a member of the APD you will have access to focused, logical and narrowcast media, it is all under the umbrella of the 'Directive'.

All of the information is within APD with the Middle Living and Superior Senior television/webcasted/radio channels as a unique driver. With this channel you have-

The APD will be mobile, flexible and truly unique. It will be proprietary and members only. In addition, it will include 'PrimeFresh', the Amazon 'Linus' project and the Amazon 'Entrepreneur's Gallery' where business coaching is trusted and shared.

I could go on, and we will, I am sure of it.

APD has many choices under its umbrella many choices, increasing the ability to fulfill your 'one thing'. Whatever your one thing is, I will bet we can find an example.

Activities, health, travel, food choices, the 'Directive' fulfills:

The Middle Living/Superior Senior demographic is living longer than any other cohort, 90-100 years old is becoming common (centenarians are the fastest growing age demographic in our country). [http://bit.ly/1KNp7LI]

Reinvention is going to happen; I call it making 'bricks', the foundational tools to build the transitional life.

With these new adult life stages comes a need for a wide range of services and products. We have just barely scratched the surface of interesting, and with new found desires in wellness, as mentioned last week, the Trillion dollar food industry dilemma is just one facet of impending change.

It is the 'What,' but more importantly it certainly will be the 'How'.

Peace

Tom

WEEK 44

Subject: Handcuffing Healthcare

July 5

From: Tom Matt

To: Jeff Bezos

Hey Jeff,

With all of the technological advances we have made in healthcare, with all of the billions of dollars spent, why then does, according to 'World Health Organization's Ranking of the World's Health Systems' the U.S. ranks 37th?

In an article by Antonio Regaldo from Business Reports he used Moore's Law to illustrate the point and major bone of contention. He stated, "Moore's Law predicts that every two years the cost of computing will fall by half. That is why we can be sure that tomorrow's gadgets will be better, and cheaper, too. But in American hospitals and doctors' offices, a very different law seems to hold sway: every 13 years, spending on U.S. health care doubles."

Ouch!

With healthcare costs at nearly 18% of GDP clearly our ranking of a paltry 37th globally is not a sustainable model. My question to you is "Why"?

My answer to the $5 Trillion dollar question is simple actually. It is the 'silver bullet' mentality. That the conditioning of our people, gadgets, Internet-style business models, drugs, and magic machines that can see inside our bodies suffice to serve all and cure all. We have removed the joy of accountability, disincentivized, and trained our citizens to disregard becoming proactive and have a vision of what healthy really is.

And it is 'handcuffing healthcare'.

Through adversity grows opportunity!

Confusion reigns supreme because of the dearth of wellness information does not help people understand that choice, balance, and what is right for the individual Genomics, Bioinformatics, Epigenetics, Integrative, Holistic, Alternative, Complementary, and Holistic medicines, along with advanced treatments and diagnostic tools. Nutraceuticals, Pharmaceuticals, Supplements, Vitamins, Whole food, Exercise, fitness, active living all add up to supreme potential, and still we grow more confused.

The U.S. ranks 11th as the healthiest nation, spending 18% of GDP does not seem to be helping us.

Until now!

Jeff, you creating Amazon, the deliverer of information is the key to unlocking the handcuffs. It has enabled a person like me to become inspired, educated, and enthusiastic about the future. And it holds the potential to enlighten and empower even more.

When I created the term Middle Living it was because of my disdain for the term 'Midlife'. Last week I pitched the idea of the 'Middle Living Minute' to a radio syndicator who is looking hard at our programming, he likes the idea and wanted me to cut a couple of demos. Being on the cutting edge is better than being on the cutting floor so we shall see. No idea is a bad idea!

Without your assistance in building the great enabler, Amazon, I would not consume the books that have given me the knowledge to help the world become a better place. You gave me the keys, I had to do my own thing, and so does everyone else. It can happen, and I am doing this, confidence and self-efficacy, Apple-Pie, Chevrolet, and American exceptionalism.

I mentioned the 'Middle Living Channel' to you before, this is just the beginning, please enjoy the promo, because when I start cutting these and producing one for every day of the week people will know, and they will have their keys to health and wellness. Placing a one minute blast on syndicated talk radio stations validates our platform, and opens the door to the future.

Loving life is power, sharing the love is the best!

Peace,

Tom

12

THE AGING PARADOX

"The future ain't what it used to be."
Yogi Berra

In the 21st century we Middle Living and Superior Seniors have a dichotomy of sorts. Our two most valuable resources are needed to play the game of life correctly and maximizing their effectiveness takes skill.

These resources are 'time' and 'information'.

Information is at its most abundant time ever in man's history. Lucky for all of us, especially the younger generations, that we Middle Living boomers invented the information age and this new-fangled thing called the Internet.

Think about this:

There are 1440 minutes per day...that means there are approximately:

- 294 BILLION emails sent every day!
- 6 BILLION Google Searches each day!
- 3.5 BILLION Facebook messages posted daily!
- 40 Million Tweets shared each day!4

That is a staggering amount of information, and it is growing!

Now consider that I plan on living to 100. Currently I am 56, so I have 44 years to go. Every day I use 86,400 seconds, my time is finite and it is shrinking. As we grow older our mortality becomes clearer, our parents'age and we eventually will lose them. Our friends will grow older, and we will lose them as well.

Our most precious resources are moving in opposite directions, time is finite and information seems infinite.

I believe in the power of knowledge and utilizing it to empower my well-being. Using information to grow wiser, healthier, and happier. I can do this by making better use of my time by staying engaged in the game of life, and employing the abundant information to its fullest. I have a new equation to illustrate this-

Choice + Challenge= Change

Try these:

Peace

The best of 'Tom Matts Boomers Rock' radio talk show discusses economic development and then some. In this episode Dr. Roger Landry, President of Master Piece Living™, author of the awesome book "Live Long, Die Short joins us for a lively conversation.

WEEK 45

Subject: Move-Sleep-Poop

July 12

From: Tom Matt

To: Jeff Bezos

Hey Jeff,

So, I go to get my hair cut this week, and as usual I always paw through the stack of magazines that are consistently piling up. I see a head shot of you in a Fast Company edition from February 2015 and of course I dive bomb the article. My stylist always allows me to pinch these old magazines so I had a chance to really get the juice from this piece.

Now this one I thought was pretty solid, I know these writers (Austin Carr for this one) gotta have their edginess; it is part of the whole creative 21st century thing. You kiss someone on the cheek all while dropping critical subconscious, or even conscious backstabbing, hey it sells right. The last three sentences of this article was just such a closer, time to again offer to offer my rebuttal. I mean, "Amazon is admired by customers for what it does, rather than loved for some iteration of itself that Bezos has clearly desired. The world doesn't need another Steve Jobs. They want Jeff Bezos, the way he used to be."

Holy backhanded face slap Batman!

Well maybe Mr. Carr needs to follow the advice of the title of this note, time to 'Move-Sleep-Poop' a little more. I for one love your creative massiveness and not being afraid to challenge yourself! I mean come on it's Jeff fricking Bezos for god's sake!

When someone in your Lab126 states from that same article that, "we can't compete head to head with Apple," that "there is a branding issue: Apple is premium, while our customers want a great product at a great price" I say,

"LIMITING BELIEFS WILL CRUSH YOUR CREATIVITY"!

or

"Get off my bus"

I have read that big data has an accepted notion that goes something like this:

First descriptive analytics, ok, then predictive analytics, uhm ok, and then prescriptive analytics, enough already! When the world is flooded with data, when it becomes difficult to extract the information that is relevant to average people then we have our opportunity to exploit the conduit of good information.

Digital data will grow by ten times by 2020, can you say a whole bunch of white noise!

Why is everything so dang complicated?

Jeff, if you want to be cool, then give people a reason to love you, because being loved is indispensable, cool is just trendy.

Think about this, really-smart-empowered-business-development-team-at-Amazon.

According to Oxford Economics, Americans over 45 will dominate the next 30 years economically, their spending habits and work-life preferences will rule the American landscape. The report stated that this demographic (Middle Living) will be responsible for nearly 100 million jobs and create over $4.5 trillion in wages and salaries.

That is a big number and Amazon can be the leader in the trend, my newest idea is called H2D dot it (H2D.It), which stands for 'How 2 Do dot It'.

I like DIY stuff, I like H2D.It more because we keep it simple, get people doing three things better, Move-Sleep-Poop, and you are not only cool and trendy, but I guarantee you will be loved. Middle Living has never seen the like of this.

H2D.It fits the Amazon Active model the Amazon Linus and the Amazon Fresh idea and of course it all falls under the Prime Directive. Great ideas meeting your non-stop innovation mindset; deliverables in every media stream imaginable.

A Middle Living channel juggernaut.

Amazon is amazing and I beg to differ with Mr. Carr again that you are an aspirational brand, you are also an enabler of living life in a whole new coachable world, a H2D dot It world!

Believe me when people embrace all of the tactics laid down by Coach Jeff and the A-team, when people simplify their lives and Move-Sleep-Poop better; there is a whole lot of lovin that will be going down.

Simple fundamentals: Get people moving, get people sleeping, get people pooping consistently and they will love you.

Everyone thinks new and crazy novel ideas are ridiculous, just like 'FitBit', 'Airbnb', or this online bookstore called 'Amazon'!

An IPhone can't do this!

Peace,

Tom

WEEK 46

Subject: Tilt

July 19

From: Tom Matt

To: Jeff Bezos

Hey Jeff,

One issue I have with staying on top of my readings is my addiction to buying books on your site, it sometimes (no sometimes about it, it does) slow me down with my magazine subscriptions. My goal this week while we were on vacation was to get through some of my ignored issues; creativity comes in the written word.

Ever heard of a young man named Marques Brownlee? Neither had I until I read about his newfound fame from the November 2014 edition of Wired, (yes I am that far behind). Apparently this 20 year old is something of a YouTube sensation due to his affinity to reviewing and testing things. His 1.8 million subscribers attest to his burgeoning fame, I say "good for you Marques!"

I feel another creative moment coming on!

Last week, remember I touched on the ever growing amount of data and information that is becoming a sea of white noise to the average person in our tribe? Bring in the Middle Living and especially the Superior Senior demographics and you have well over 100 million, (more like 150 but hey big numbers right) you have the pinball equivalent of "Tilt".

Remember "Tilt", when the pinball machine went dead because you were pushing, leaning and rattling its cage to hard? That is what is happening to people over the age of 45 with the tidal wave of information, 'Tilt'!

Hmmm, smart-empowered-business-development-pepes-at-Amazon this one is for you. Put it on a tee and drill that bad boy. See a problem, solve a problem, and capture the flag!

In one of my earlier 45 emails (please remember my goal is 52) I mentioned to you about the beauty of your Amazon review process, of the at least 300 books I have bought on your site, (give or take 50) the review process is critical. It is empowering and adds to my addiction, it also has enabled my radio program to become syndicated, however more on that another time.

Keeping in mind that Marques Brownlee, a 20 year old, can garner 1.8 million followers of his channel, here is this week's development idea.

The Amazon Middle Living Channel presents 'Tilt', a new conduit of information, similar to the radio talk show that cuts through the bull crap, is fed by submissions, and is a platform for everyone that is growing a little bit older. You name it, we talk about it, review it, crunch it and everyone else joins the party too!

This is a feeder to join the 'Prime-Directive', become one with 'Amazon-Active', and create solutions.

Ask a millennial what tilt means and they are thinking leaning or something. Ask a Middle Living and or a Superior Senior adult and they will remember pinball and 'Tilt'.

I bet you did!

Short and sweet, Jeff, lean on the machine too hard and you lose your round on the pinball machine. Cut through the clutter, give options, and empower.

It is perfect, just like H2D.it

With "How 2 Do.it" it is a lesson, with 'Tilt' it is a game show of sorts with an embedded mission, get it?

Peace,

Tom

WEEK 47

Subject: Never Become Hopeless

July 26

From: Tom Matt

To: Jeff Bezos

Hey Jeff,

Hopeless is defined as 'inadequate, or incompetent, causing despair about something', to me the word hurts my gut. Life is a tough road, and being hopeless is cause for interdiction. It is the compelling why for all of what I do.

Think of this, life is like standing in the batter's box facing a Major Leaguer, frightening, exciting, intimidating, and fun. You could also say it is exasperating. From a high hard one to a sweeping curve, to a blazing plate painter or a dancing knuckle ball and a dropping off a cliff sinker in the dirt, the thought of just stepping up is knee-buckling. Life can send you to the dugout as fast as Aroldis Chapman can smoke three past you. It is the training and practice that gives birth to confidence. The more times we step up the more times we become better, the more times we seek coaching the feeling of inadequacy can disappear.

On Coach JB's team the saying is, "through adversity grows opportunity!"

As we all grow older and the carousel of life spins on for years and years we lose the sense of adventure, change, and growth. Hopelessness creeps into our lives, that is, if we allow it.

Jeff for the first twenty years of my adult life, 18 to 38 years old I was on that carousel. Always functional and never getting into trouble, but slowly I slipped into a pattern. Social drug use, and abusive drinking habits led to dropping out of college, a dysfunctional marriage, divorce, single parenthood, and hopelessness. It took looking into the mirror and stepping up and not liking how I was swinging my bat to realize that accountability was the only way.

This is what fuels the journey now, knowing that there are many others who are suffering silently in their own hopelessness of a life that could have been.

I am going to do what I can to help others understand and realize that through my story you can take my 'left-turns' and make it right.

Confidence is built on the foundation of practice, desire, determination and focus but it all comes down to one thing, choice. No one will force you to stand in the batter's box against the grizzled steely eyed veteran, it is your decision, your life.

People can regret mistakes, but you never want to think of yourself as a 'loser', because becoming accountable takes as much guts as standing in that batter's box.

Losers don't fight, they quit.

Choose the right thing, make an informed intelligent decision.

Re-building of a generation or two will take collaboration, effort, and a positive attitude. It will take kicking limiting beliefs to the curb and building faith. It will take inspiring dreams and goals. It will take stories of overcoming poor swings and strike-outs. It will take great coaching and leadership, but most importantly it will take mentoring others, giving and loving, sharing success and desire.

Nothing in this world is unachievable, you just have to do the right things, work hard, and keep swinging.

Hopelessness does not build a better society, hope does.

Through adversity grows opportunity!

Peace,

Tom

WEEK 48

Subject: It's Called A-Squared

August 2

From: Tom Matt

To: Jeff Bezos

Hey Jeff,

In a recent article in The Wall Street Journal, Sara Germano wrote that in a survey from the Physical Activity Council, 1 in 4 Americans did not exercise at all in the past year.

Yes, according to the article 28% had not done any type of exercise, AT ALL!

As I have said many times, "through adversity grows opportunity". It sounds like it is time for the Middle Living/Superior Senior demographics to lead a new mindset. We need to teach, instruct, and lead by example in the area of fun, and activities that promote movement.

How will we do this?

Say hello to 'A-Squared!'

Planting ideas, like so many Johnny Appleseed apple trees 'A-Squared' covers the gamut of media distribution, all under the same 'A-Squared' umbrella. From television to books, radio to everyday one minute online video, from apps to articles, from web delivered or mail delivered, we got you covered. 'A-Squared' cares and listens, it provides hope and fun. It provides incentivization because it is like the great amusement park, lots of thrills and fun, and you get to choose what to do.

Watch, listen, read, live gigs, services, training, education, certifications, products, just about anything.

Massive choice, great ideas, supreme examples, great value add. All improving the QOL for millions, leadership is based on being a great talent scout, leadership is based on caring.

On September 28th, 1953 a 39 year old change agent began a new concept on a new medium. Exercise on television, a fifteen minute shot in the dark, a show which was a filler between the morning news and a cooking show. That show would run for 34 years and become the longest running exercise program on television. It would spawn countless books, devices, and attention. The man was an idol of mine, his name was Jack LaLanne.

Jack was a pioneer and a leader. The time has come for the next generational changing idea to help millions. 'A-Squared'.

By leading by example and walking through the front door of the "ReFirement Zone" we make this happen.

The number of completely sedentary Americans has risen 18% since 2007. Experts are concerned that decreasing minutes for gym class in schools is a chief contributor to rising levels of inactivity among adults.

Ever heard of 'Tag' or 'Red-Rover'!

In 1984 at the age of 70, handcuffed, shackled, and fighting strong winds and currents, Jack LaLanne towed 70 rowboats, one with several guests, from the Queen's Way Bridge in the Long Beach Harbor to the Queen Mary. It was a distance of 1 mile.

70 years old, and that was 1984!

Time to lead; how many of us remember playing touch football in the street, Red Light, Green Light or Hide and Seek?

Find a need, fulfill the need, and lead by example, 'A-Squared', it's not a diet plan, it's a generational altering lifestyle.

70 rowboats, really?

Peace,

Tom

13

BELIEVE IN AMAZING

When you have confidence, you can have a lot of fun. And when you have fun, you can do amazing things.
Joe Namath

Ok everyone, time for a New Year's resolution brain shift, and since it is August why not think about it now.

I have never been a huge fan of 'New Years Day resolutions.

First, the number one New Year's Resolution for 2015 was to lose weight, that one is out the window!

So much for New Year's day, huh!

When we start to 'Believe in Amazing' weight loss is not our primary goal. And since only 8% of people are actually successful at their resolutions, we need a paradigm shift anyway. Now we focus on our body image and how we feel, so to 'Believe in Amazing' for 2016 the goal is one of three things.

I am liking the thought of 'Well-Being'. My goal is to just feel great and do the small things that will help me get there. 47% of people make a resolution with self improvement and or educational related resolutions, fabulous! With our new emphasis on 'Believing in Amazing' and incremental change, (smaller goals are achievable goals) we are going to change the way we think about the New Year and the new you and me.

I love the thought of 'Self-Improvement' and 'Educational' resolutions!

A large number of people, 38%, make weight related resolutions, again when we reframe our resolution goals to 'Believe Amazing' and weight becomes a non-factor, feeling better is.

Try these-

Peace

Our final best of 'Tom Matts Boomers Rock' radio talk show episodes features educator, coach, long term friend and just plain great guy Scott Warriner. I could not think of a better last episode to insert into this book than this conversation with Scott. The need that is in the world for multi-generational education is a primary topic, please listen and think about how you can hjelp yourself while helping young people make our world a better place.

WEEK 49

Subject: Why Average Sucks!

August 9

From: Tom Matt

To: Jeff Bezos

Hey Jeff,

Jim Collins' classic book Good to Great is written with a premise that business, (and through osmosis the people involved in those businesses) is accepting that good is ok and we have lost the ability and or drive to find greatness.

I want to take that a couple of steps further.

I believe that we have an energy problem in our country, and I am not referring to high octane fuel, I am talking about people and performance. That in a bulk of corporate America we basically go through the motions, and that is accepted as ok. That being average is ok, that being mediocre is acceptable and even being in the walking dead of showing up is tolerated. As this occurs, happiness wanes, personal achievement is lost, and high performance and love for the work disappears.

Time for a reality check!

In Dean Tucker's book Using the Power of Purpose, a survey of employees yielded this:

Hmmmm,

So let's put these percentages into play, let's use a baseball team (9 players) for example:

Basically betting on that team is a big fat loser!

When American business pays a lot of money and benefits to receive somewhere between 15% and 37% of effort and capacity, it's time to reevaluate the situation. As reported in The New York Times, "a 2010 study, James K. Harter and colleagues found that lower job satisfaction foreshadowed poorer bottom line performance. Gallup estimates the cost of America's disengagement crisis at a staggering $300 billion in lost productivity annually."

Reigniting your life takes thought, planning, and building a foundation. Transitional careers take coaching and energy.

You following me here, coach JB?

Middle Living adults make up by far the largest group of entrepreneurs in our country. Share positive energy through ideas, lessons, coaching, and examples through various media streams (giving people a choice is the key), and you got a huge number of potentials.

It comes down to emotional energy and excitement because it is virtually impossible to get high output from very low input. Peter Koestenbaum writes in his book 'Leadership' that, "85% of organizational effectiveness and industrial competitiveness can be attributed to moral, spirit, and heart, and to the commitment and loyalty employees give to their companies, to that inventiveness, imagination and creativity they devote to their jobs".

Creating positivity, (my whole purpose with everything I now do), brings everything to my work. Innovation, creativity, caring, enabling beliefs, generosity of spirit, massively huge ideas and the energy to make the extra effort worth-while is the difference between average and great.

Igniting lives matters, making a difference matters, helping others matters, but what matters most is having the enthusiasm to believe that anything is possible.

Anything IS possible, you just gotta BELIEVE!

Peace,

Tom

WEEK 50

Subject: The Wellness Paradigm

August 16

From: Tom Matt

To: Jeff Bezos

Hey Jeff,

I am preparing for a keynote speech that will be hosted at Michigan State University on November 10th of this year (2015), which you will certainly be invited to. The Eli Broad Executive Development program at MSU hosts monthly forums which is called 'Business and Bagels'. The title of my program is "Ignite Your Life: Self-Improvement, Leadership and the Wellness Paradigm."

Wellness is an active process of becoming aware of and making choices toward a healthy and fulfilling life. It is one of the fastest growing segments in business and employee cost savings. Empowering others to see the potential of living a successful happier and fulfilled life starts with the mindset that wellness is the path. There is only one problem, the information super-highway is choked with information, making informed choices is complicated, confusing, and difficult.

See a problem, create a solution, I like to say Coach JB!

For many corporations, wellness programs offer 'the greatest opportunity to both control and reduce costs and enhance the quality of life enjoyed by members of the workforce.' (Wang 1997)

Why are we handcuffing our healthcare providers and in essence creating our own demise?

See a problem, create a service and content to educate our people. Give them a conduit of good information, create 'The Wellness Para-

digm' television program delivered on the Middle Living Channel brought to you exclusively by the
'Amazon Prime-Directive'.

There are eight dimensions of wellness as defined by the University of California Davis, which are:

1. Emotional
2. Intellectual
3. Environmental
4. Physical
5. Spiritual
6. Social
7. Financial
8. Occupational

https://shcs.ucdavis.edu/wellness/#.VWJuik9Viko

I then will throw just a little bit of science related medical advances that can change the face of health and wellness. These include:

And the beat goes on, and on and on!

No wonder we are rated number 11 on the healthiest nation chart, how can anyone decide anything when contraindications, confusion, and flat out indecisiveness reign supreme?

Find a problem and then assist others in helping with consistent information. Building trust, education, stories of success, and just plain discussing all of this is a good place to start.

The 'Wellness Paradigm' is a golden opportunity, I want to learn and share the truth, the radio program, my live events, and articles all touch on all of this constantly. Collaborate with a leader and share ideas, it really does do a body and nation good.

Peace,

Tom

WEEK 51

Subject: The Subjectivity of 'Age'

August 23

From: Tom Matt

To: Jeff Bezos

Hey Jeff,

When you see headlines that try and convince people that 60 is the new 40, or 70 is the new 50, or 50 is the new 30, I get a tad irritated. Ok, if you would like to quantify these 'new' mindsets by adding subjective to the term now I can get my head around the whole paradigm. The title is 'Subjectivity' right, it is how you think because in the past it was 65 and out and dead, make sense?

Growing older is perfectly normal, feeling good about like life is in itself great, looking back and quantifying, is, in itself not. Personally with all of the left turns, poor decisions, negative behaviors, and growing up I had to do, looking back is just what fuels my looking forward. Looking back for me is the catalyst to the 'new-new' me, it lets help others see in this way. Many people are in similar situations, they just need stories and examples to fuel their personal feelings of subjective aging.

Having a 'subjective 'rather than 'objective' mindset into aging potential is a precursor to happiness and well-being. Accountability is the only way that we can alleviate the stress on our legacy systems, such as insurance, healthcare and governmental programs. I believe that those legacy systems are going to strain us to keep up. Insightful thinking into subjective aging has the potential to help us improve quality of life for an ageing population and ease these burdens.

See a problem, fix the problem. I think you may have heard this before from me, Coach JB.

There are studies that have shown that lowering your subjective age, in fact, improves quality of life. Behaving and living with a subjective mindset in turn has the potential of reducing health issues and even adding to lifespan, according to the researchers. Just because your body numerically says you are 75, 65 or 55 does not mean squat, it is how you subjectively view your life, how you act and how you behave. I like to use the term "activities that promote movement that are fun" in place of exercise and fitness. Those people who are connected, technologically, socially, physically ,and spiritually tend to utilize their time more effectively, and in turn are happier, live life with a sense of empowered quality of life.

The positive subjective aging experiences are very diverse and can affect not only interpersonal relationships, but educational and professional development. Growing older does not mean you stop living, hardly, what it can mean is the liberation of creative and positive energies and synergies. Stories of successful aging are desired, are Prime examples of the doability of change.

Creating and delivering the finest narrowcast content through multiple delivery streams is the next big, big thing.

The potential through what we deliver as ambassadors and media entrepreneurs is as what Captain Kirk from Star Trek would say, "a new frontier!"

I am going to use this creative opportunity to continue our transitional career, when you build an all-star team you need an all-star manager. You also need an owner who is willing to take chances and build foundations, strength comes from consistency, it also comes from hard work and effort. All of it starts with a spark, and then ... the universe is a big place. Just ask Captain Kirk, or for that matter, coach JB!

The 'Prime-Directive' is empowerment!

Peace,

Tom

ps-
Yes I did see the New York Times article on the sour grape wielding former employees, slicing and dicing Amazon this past week. This

is nothing new and I wrote you about this before. My take, "get a fricking life" scumbags!

WEEK 52

Subject: It Really is About the People

August 30

From: Tom Matt

To: Jeff Bezos

Hey Jeff,

This week my first grandson was born, truly a blessing! He is our second grandchild, Harper, our granddaughter is now a big sister, and she is now two and a half. Life really does come down to 'The Circle of Life'.

As my wife Sandy and I sat in the waiting room of Appleton, Wisconsin's St. Elizabeth hospital, Friday August 28th a lullaby played over the paging system at 2:51 pm central standard time. Baby boy, Brecken Henry Schutte had arrived!

Our first grandson and we were actually there to be part of his first few minutes on Earth.

The Circle of Life.

Brecken's birth on the last week of my 'Notes to Jeff' year-long odyssey actually is kinda surreal. To show the world that we can work together to leave a legacy of hope and share the love of our human race, and work as a collective family is beautiful. Together we make the change happen, together we improve the world for coming generations.

The time has come for us, people, to come together and overcome, break the chains of marginalization and grow strong together. Stepping up will take controversial, maybe even outlandish dreams. Making reality out of stardust, now that's a lullaby.

The Circle of Life.

In his book Humans are Underrated Geoff Colvin shares some truly remarkable theories and thoughts about people, the 21st century, work and technology. Geoff stated "ask employers which skills they'll need in the next five to ten years, as the Towers Watson consulting firm and the Oxford Economics research firm did, and the answers that come back do not include business acumen, analysis, or P&L management-left-brain thinking skills. Instead, employers' top priorities include relationship building, teaming, co-creativity, brainstorming, cultural sensitivity, and the ability to manage diverse employees-right-brain skills of social interaction."

Of course, you do have to read the tea leaves, stats are just that, stats, but it certainly is the proverbial tipping point, as Geoff went on to state, "the overall trend is a giant employment increase based on personal interaction," and that, "interaction jobs have become the fastest growing category of employment in the advanced economies."

The Circle of Life!

How you deliver a message is actually more important than the message itself, verbal communication, face to face interaction cuts through the confusion and asynchronous misreading of the thought. If you cannot stand up and talk, deliver an eye-ball to eye-ball dissection of an idea, then 'Houston we have a Problem'!

Helping the circle of life to continue to proliferate, enabling, enhancing, sharing, training, teaching, inspiring, motivating, and leading is what will make you the indispensable leader of the 21st century.

You just need to see the need and embrace the challenge. Are you feeling the juice coach JB?

There are millions of people who want to live with dignity and quality of life, however they lack the coaching, the confidence, and the plan.

All we have got to do is show true leadership!

Geoff Colvin also stated that, "humans working in groups are more crucial to the success of organizations, (I would insert civilization here personally), and whole economies, and the ability to work in groups is more crucial to the success of individuals".

The Circle of Life.

We need to encourage the focus on the other gal and other guy. We need to share the stories that can ignite lives, empower multigenerational collaboration, cooperation, and love. We need to understand that becoming the catalyst can in itself be a liberating and enabling. The time has come to break the mold of how work is done and how people view living.

Through adversity grows opportunity. The circle of life is a beautiful thing, with the right friends, mentors, and collaborators. However THE most important attribute is having the right attitude.

The Circle of Life.

Peace,

Tom

PS

Jeff,

During this odyssey of 52 notes there have been Amazing Amazon moments as I like to think of them. Momentum is building, our family is growing, people are becoming healthier, we are helping more and more in our outreach, syndication of the radio program starts next week, which will enhance our multi-media outreach! Amazing Amazon moments, who would have ever thought that making a goal of 52 weeks of ideas, thoughts, dreams, accomplishments would come to fruition. The few people I did share this project and goal of writing to you with thought I was looney; which in some aspects I am, so what! Dreamer, yes, open minded, for sure, dynamic and happy, well I will let the readers of this book be the judge, because just when they say it's a goofy outrageous idea, well.

Tell that one to a guy named Jeff Bezos, a man I admire and wrote 52 weeks of emails.

Here is to the world, here is to self-improvement, here is to loving our lives, families, friends, work and play. Here is hope to everyone to maximize their quality of life.

Thank you for reading and being part of a solution, and thank you Alice (Powers) for believing in me!

14

IN CLOSING

Writing this book was a creative journey, and you probably realized that my goal of 400 words or less in each email quickly disappeared. I did try my best to keep things tight and concise, again creativity won that one.

Also some of the original emails were slightly modified, very, very slightly. In trying to stay within the spirit of an email, (I did write most of these in one sitting with very little if any editing) to clarify some of the points our editor Josh Raab won that battle. On some of the points I stayed in my own creative mindset and let it go. Originality and realness are important to me and I wanted the reader to feel like I was talking to them, just as I was talking to Jeff.

Josh Raab did an excellent job of helping the voice stand on its own ledge, and I give him tremendous credit because as a baby boomer I understand our paradigm. Josh however is not a boomer and for him to feel the process, the message and flow was I am sure very difficult at times.

My dream with all of this is to spark creativity, to engage people and the opportunities that life holds for us. Many people doubted I would fulfill my goal, hell I doubted it myself, but as you and I both know goals can be achieved.

My love of people is the reason I do what I do. Because it took me 40 years of my life to begin to become what I was capable of, and through the love and mentorship of others I started the journey of self-improvement. Paying it forward is a humbling and exhilarating experience, and the more we all discover the potential the closer we all come to Abraham Maslows pinnacle of self-actualization.

Help others, give back, work hard and don't screw people over and you have a chance at something awesome. I look forward to hearing from any and all of the readers of this book. I am truly, truly humbled anytime my work positively impacts another soul.

To reach me directly please email me, tom@boomersrock.us. Heck I figured if Jeff Bezos can put his email in a book then I better step up too!

1 www.alz.org/annual_report/overview.asp

2 http://www.nejm.org/doi/full/10.1056/NEJMsa1204629

3 http://bit.ly/1qQEnBK

4 https://www.gwava.com/blog/internet-data-created-daily-2014

How Can We Help?

Boomers Rock can help your organization, your team, or individuals with inspiration and advice on health, fitness, leadership, and wellness. Contact Tom – Tom@BoomersRock.us – for more information.

Listen to a Show or Podcast

If you're in Michigan, you can hear Boomers Rock on

- WGHN in Grand Haven
- WJIM in Lansing
- WJRW in Grand Rapids
- WMMI in Mt. Pleasant, Michigan
- WKLQ in White Hall/Muskegon
- Spartan Sports Network Stream
- iTunes or Stitcher
- www.boomersrock.us

Speaking Engagements

Tom has developed a series of talks called Ignite Your Life! that will help you master the skills necessary to overcome any obstacle.

Learn from the Boomers Rock Library

Read one of the books from the Boomers Rock catalog:

- Maximize Your Quality of Life—The 200% Solution
- Ignite Your Life
- Attracting Abundance

Available from Amazon.com.

ABOUT TOM MATT

Tom Matt is a small town Michigan boy who grew up an average American kid. Like so many, he never took his talents seriously. Unfortunately, bad habits gave way to damaging substance addictions. He married, had a daughter, but his lifestyle led to divorce and more change.

Tom realized that he had a serious issue with alcohol and sought help to change his ways. He moved back to Michigan with his daughter and began to live the life he was meant to enjoy.

In 1999, sober and starting to build back his health, Tom reconnected with a high school sweetheart whom he married in 2001. Change begat change, and Tom enrolled at Michigan State University, earning both Bachelor and Masters degrees in Telecommunication Information Studies and Management.

Convinced that fitness leads to improved quality of life, Tom pursued a personal training certification with the National Academy of Sports Medicine. While completing that program, Tom competed in the Flint All Natural Body Building contest in Flint Michigan, in April of 2010 and, as a rookie competitor, placed 3rd in the Grand Master category, utilizing only whole foods and strength training.

In 2011, Tom created the tallk show "Boomers Rock" and has since then interviewed dozens of experts in the field of fitness, nutrition, finance, and brain health. His personal mission is to help others improve the quality of their life. And who better to counsel those seeking help than someone who has made the mistake of venturing into the darkest tunnels life offers, but who found his way out and became a new man during the journey.

The Boomers Rock Talk Show with Tom Matt can now be heard on five radio stations. All of his shows can be heard as a podcast. Visit www.boomersrock.us/listen/ to find your most convenient podcast platform.

To improve your life today, visit: www.boomersrock.us.